Rediscover *the* Saints

MERRY CHRISTMAS from all of us at St. Nicholas & St. William Catholic Parish! Hope you enjoy this book by Matthew Kelly.

As an ongoing gift for the year we have a special gift for you and your family.
THE BEST CATHOLIC CONTENT ALL IN ONE PLACE
FORMED.org/signup
Select St. Nicholas 473 Lincoln Ave Los Altos
Register with your Name and email address

MATTHEW KELLY

BLUE SPARROW
North Palm Beach, Florida

BLUE
sparrow

The First Saint was written by Father Bob Sherry
and adapted for this volume by the author.

Designed by Ashley Wirfel

For more information visit:
www.MatthewKelly.com

10 9 8 7 6 5 4 3 2 1

Printed in the United States of America

Table of Contents

. . . .

PROLOGUE:
The First Saint

. . . .

THEY SAY when the sun rises you never know how a day will end, and I have to say that I could not have imagined how some of my days ended—one in particular.

I never felt good about stealing. Breaking the law and hurting innocent people didn't bring me any joy, but I figured it was either them or me. The thing is, I was so hungry, and the bread or the fish or the meat was right there in front of me. I knew if I didn't take it I would die, and I wasn't going to let that happen. I suppose we all have that basic survival instinct, but most of the people who judge people like me have never been on the razor's edge of survival. It breeds desperation, and desperate people do desperate things.

So, I did what I had to do. I became a thief.

Everybody was always better off than I was. My mother died when I was four, and my father threw me out to fend for myself when I was five, and from that day on, stealing food became a daily priority. I wanted to live. I was young but I still knew it was wrong, so I would justify it to myself. "They have plenty; they won't miss one piece of fish." "It's not the difference between life and death for them. They will live and so will I."

Stealing one fish led to stealing two fish. Then one day I saw an amazing bowl of fruit and I stole that. Eating fruit made me want bread and wine and all the things the rich people ate. But I quickly discovered that a guy needs more than just food. "Aren't I entitled to a little more?" I asked myself, and before too long I was stealing all sorts of things: clothes, sandals, a cart . . . even a donkey. It turned out I was a good thief.

I told myself that it wouldn't be forever—but we tell ourselves so many things, don't we? I thought that someday I would change and find a way to make an honest living. But one thing leads to the next, and this is how the years pass.

When I was fifteen I started to think that if I was getting away with this much in a small town, why not move up to a village or even a city? This got me wondering what sorts of amazing things might be in those places, and a few months later I was on my way.

As I arrived in the first village a thought crossed my mind. "Nobody knows me here. Nobody knows I am a thief. This is my chance to start afresh." I thought about getting a job and making an honest living. But then the doubts began to fill my mind. "Who are you kidding? The only thing you know how to do is steal." I pushed that thought out of my mind and said to myself, "You could get good at something else, something respectable."

But later that night my stomach began to growl. I had been walking all day and once again my hunger got the better of me. The sun was setting and the traders were packing up their goods in the marketplace, which is a perfect time to steal because they aren't paying attention.

It wasn't long before I had a reputation as a thief just like I'd had in my hometown. That's when I decided to make my way to the big city. Some people called it Jerusalem and others called it the City of David. I had once asked a man in the marketplace when I was younger, "Who was David and why do they call it his city?" But he laughed at me and turned back to his conversation, muttering, "Didn't your parents teach you anything?"

When I arrived in Jerusalem I was amazed. I had never seen anything like it. There were so many people and so many traders, and trades I had never thought about. People spent their whole lives making pots or tables, carts or even lanterns. I had never really thought about where those things came from, but there it dawned on me that real people make them.

Once again that thought filled my mind: "Nobody knows me here. Nobody knows I am a thief. This is my chance to start afresh." My heart swelled with hope that maybe, just maybe, I could turn my life around. I had a few coins, so I would not be hungry tonight; I could buy food like an honest man. That night I fell asleep dreaming about how good it would be not to always feel anxious about getting recognized and caught. "I have been anxious and afraid my whole life," I thought, and the idea of putting all that behind me made me feel light and happy.

The next day I went to apply for a job, first as a pot maker, then as a carpenter, and next at the place where they made lanterns. But all the foremen sent me away, saying I didn't have any experience.

But my hope was still alive and I had a little money still, so I bought myself some food and again fell asleep hoping for a better life.

For days I went from one trader to the next asking for a chance. "I'll do anything," I said to them, but they sent me away. I didn't know anything about fishing or making wine or tending animals. How could I? "Life is not fair!" I started thinking to myself . . . again. I had told myself this my whole life.

Each day I had fewer coins left in the worn purse I had stolen many years ago, and the fear and anxiety began to creep back into my heart. It wasn't long before I was back to doing the only thing I had ever known.

I remember the first day I got back to stealing. My purse was empty and I was sad. I knew what I was going to do, I knew what I needed to do to survive, but I didn't want to do it. While I was feeling sorry for myself I saw a huge crowd. My instincts kicked in; crowds are good for thieving.

Making my way through the crowd looking for someone to target, I realized they were listening to one of those itinerant preachers. "The sun shines on the just and the unjust alike," I heard him say. Words, words, words, just words. In my cynicism I thought to myself, "They sound good, but right now the sun sure isn't shining down on me."

A few days later I saw the same man, and I overheard someone call him the son of David. There was no crowd this time, just a small group of about twelve men, so I moved a little closer and heard one of the men ask him, "Lord, if another man wrongs me, how many times should I forgive him? Seven?" The preacher smiled and said, "I know seven times seems more than just, even generous. But I tell you, you should forgive him seventy-seven times." The men gathered around him were astonished. I was astonished too, but because I knew people were not like that. Then he started talking about his kingdom, a kingdom that was not of this world, where people could live forever. None of this made any sense to me, so I wandered off.

The days passed and I reluctantly went back to doing whatever I had to just to survive, but it was harder than ever to steal. My heart wasn't in it. I yearned for something else, something different, something more. I longed to go to sleep every night as peaceful and unafraid as I had been that first night in Jerusalem. But the fear and the anxiety of the poor began to dominate my heart again.

The following spring the city came to life in a way I had never seen it. "The pilgrims are coming for the celebration in the temple," I heard people say. One night as I was eating at my favorite inn I heard another thief say, "During the festival I will be able to steal enough gold, silver, and denarii to take care of my family for a year."

A new hope began to rise up in me. If I could get such a haul I could stop stealing and try again to find something respectable to do. For months, I would be able to go to bed with hope each night like I had that first night in Jerusalem.

As the crowds made their way into the city for the celebrations, I noticed a wealthy trader. I followed him for a few days, learning his routines, and noticed that he had a chest of coins that he opened with a key each morning to take out what he needed for the day.

I waited patiently for the right moment. I was confident because I was a good thief. It was probably the only thing I had ever been good at. The next morning after the trader had left for the day I approached his caravan. There was the chest. I felt bad about taking it all, but I had to get away as quickly as possible. I picked up the chest and it was much heavier than I expected. My heart soared with hope that this might be the last time I had to steal. Wrapping the chest in an old cloak, I tucked it under my arm and turned around to leave. My heart sank. Three Roman soldiers were standing there watching, waiting, and that was the end of my life as a thief. They arrested me and threw me in prison.

I sat there in prison thinking about my life. I had regrets, but I had done what I had to do to survive. I had tried to walk a better path, but life can be so cruel. At that moment I looked up and I saw one of the guards talking to his son. They were smiling and laughing, and then the father took his son in his arms, hugged him, and tousled his hair.

I began to cry. I was so surprised at my reaction; I hadn't cried since I was a boy. At first, I didn't know why I was crying, but then a shaft of light crossed my face and it occurred to me. Nobody had ever talked to me like that father spoke to his son. Nobody had ever laughed and smiled with me like that father did with his son. Nobody had ever hugged me like he hugged his boy. Nobody had ever, in my whole life, tousled my hair like that soldier had tousled his son's hair. And the thing is, it seemed so natural.

I thought about my life and I thought about how different that boy's life was from mine and I wondered . . . I wondered so many things. . . .

The next thing I knew, the guards were waking me. I must have fallen asleep. It was time. The Romans crucified thieves and it was my turn.

They took me and another thief, Gestas, to a small hill outside the city to crucify us. I had heard of this place and had always avoided it, but there was no avoiding it now.

I would die as I had lived, anxious and afraid. That thought was interrupted by a commotion. It was another criminal and a rowdy crowd. But when I looked closely at him I realized it was that son of David person. "What did he do?" I thought to myself.

I would die as I had lived, anonymous and ignored. Everyone was looking at the preacher; nobody cared that I was about to die. There were women crying and I heard someone say one of the women was this man's mother. For the first time in my life I was glad my mother was dead. I wouldn't have wanted her here. No mother should have to see her son die.

The soldiers nailed us each to a wooden cross. The pain was excruciating. "Why are men so cruel to each other?" I thought. Then the other thief, Gestas, cried out, "Jesus, look at me." I had heard that name. He had been doing miracles and people had been saying he was the Messiah. Was this really him? What had he done to deserve this? As a criminal you get to know other criminals, and it was clear to me that this man Jesus was no criminal.

The other thief kept taunting Jesus, mocking him, ridiculing him, and some of the crowd joined in. "I thought you were the Christ," Gestas said. "If you are the Christ, prove it. Save yourself and while you're at it, save us!"

The guards had been much crueler to Jesus than they had been to me, and I could see he was in agony. "Shut up, Gestas!" I found myself saying. "What has he done wrong? We are getting what we deserve, but he hasn't done anything to deserve this." At that moment I felt Jesus looking at me. I was suffocating, but I raised my eyes to meet his, and he looked at me like nobody had ever looked at me before. It was the first time in my life that I felt like anyone really saw me. And he had this look in his eyes that said, "Everything is going to be all right."

It was a moment like no other in my life; he was a man like no other man I had ever known or even heard about, and I said to him, "Jesus, remember me when you come into your kingdom."

As he looked at me, I thought he was trying to smile, and then he said, "I promise you, today you will be with me in paradise."

Today I hear people calling me Saint Dismas. It seemed strange to me the first time I heard it, but Jesus and death and eternity have taught me that God's ways are gloriously different from the ways of man.

They say every saint has a past and every sinner has a future. If I could lean in close to you and whisper something in your ear, it would be this: "If there are pieces of your past that are weighing you down, it's time to leave them behind. You are not what has happened to you. You are someone unimaginably greater than you have ever considered, and maybe it's time to consider all the possibilities that are within you."

GETTING STARTED:
Amazing Possibilities

. . . .

WE ARE CAPABLE of so much more than we think. You have no idea what you are capable of. None of us do. God is constantly trying to open our eyes to the amazing possibilities that he has enfolded in our being. The saints continue this work, encouraging us to explore all our God-given potential, not with speeches but with the example of their lives.

When we have the courage to collaborate with God and pursue our truest self, he lights a fire within us that is so bright and warm, it keeps shining long after our days on this earth have come to an end. The lives of the saints have captivated the people of every age for this very reason.

There are two questions that confront the people of every place and time, questions that confront you and me today: Are you satisfied with the direction the world is moving in? Are you satisfied with your life?

These questions are always before us, within us, around us.

They are part of our spiritual quest and part of our human quest. These questions linger in our minds when we read the news of happenings in our own country and around the world. They tickle our souls when we witness the battle between good and evil, however it manifests in our own lives.

Are you satisfied with the direction the world is moving in? This is one of life's inescapable questions, and we each respond with passionate action or selfish indifference. Our collective dissatisfaction with the direction of the world leads to the consensus that the world needs changing. And yet we seem gripped by exasperation and paralyzed by the false belief that we can't do anything about it. The saints dispel that exasperation and inspire us to bold action. They remind us over and over again: We can change the world.

What does the world need? It needs holy moments. That's all. The solution is usually simpler than we imagine. History is a collection of holy moments and unholy moments. Our desire to see the world change is a desire to see the holy moments outweigh the unholy.

What is a holy moment? A holy moment is a moment when you make yourself completely available to God. You set self-interest aside, you set aside what you want to do or feel like doing, and for that moment you do exactly what you sense God is calling you to do. The saints were masterful at taking the ordinary, everyday events of life and turning them into holy moments.

The biggest mistake we can make when it comes to the saints is to think of them as different. Our desire to put them on pedestals and venerate them is driven by positive and negative motives. On one hand we want to celebrate their goodness; on the other hand we want to set them apart as different because doing so absolves us of our responsibility to live as boldly and passionately as they did. But the brilliant and beautiful truth is you are just as capable of collaborating with God to create holy moments as the saints were.

Another mistake we can make is to lose ourselves in our quest to imitate the saints. The world doesn't need another Francis of Assisi or Mother Teresa or Ignatius of Loyola or Thérèse of Lisieux. The world needs you. The world needs the-very-best-version-of-you, fully alive and collaborating with God every day to create as many holy moments as possible.

Writing a book about the saints has been a daunting task. There are so many books already, and I didn't see any sense in writing yet another collection of short biographies of saints. There are dozens of those types of books. So, you will not find that here. I wanted to do something unique. I hope it feeds you, encourages you, challenges you, and inspires you to live life in new and exciting ways. And if a particular saint touches your heart and captures your imagination, I hope you will delve deeper into that saint's life by reading her writings or a biography of his life.

The saints are great teachers, primarily because they teach with their actions as much as with their words. Their lives raise questions about our lives, and when we ponder those questions, amazing possibilities begin to unfold within and around us.

The saints are always there, swirling around us. They intersect our lives at unexpected times in unexpected ways, but they always come bearing a question or an answer, sometimes both. The saints teach us, encourage us, challenge us, and inspire us. I wish I had more friends like them.

The saints show us what is possible, and what is possible is amazing. You are capable of incredible things. Don't be afraid to embrace your beautiful self. The more you do so, the more others will also. Do not be afraid of possibilities. There are always so many more than the ones you see easily. Take time to reflect. Look deeper. Seek out the unseen opportunities that you have overlooked at first glance. Possibilities abound. You and I—human beings—are capable of incredible things.

There will be fabulous joy in the journey, as well as heart-wrenching pain. Anyone who offers you an easy path is to be mistrusted. Life is difficult and messy; there is no point trying to mask that or pretend otherwise. But every situation you encounter is in need of one thing: a holy moment.

We underestimate ourselves, but God never does. He knows exactly what you are capable of in collaboration with him. Allow God to raise up the saint in you. This is what your corner of the world needs right now.

1. AUGUSTINE:
You Have a Future

. . . .

***What do you believe about your past that is
keeping you from your future?***

"**EVERY SAINT** has a past and every sinner has a future." This
was Oscar Wilde's observation. Wherever you are in your journey, wherever you have been and whatever you have done, the
lives of saints such as Augustine remind us that God never gives
up on us—even if at times we give up on ourselves or give up
on him.

Augustine had given himself over to just about every pleasure
and ambition that this world has to offer, but they all left him dissatisfied. His own words sum up his journey and his destination in
a single line: "Our hearts are restless Lord, until they rest in you."

We all have restless hearts. How often have we fallen into the
trap of thinking the things of this world are more important
than they are? How often have we mistakenly believed that certain things, pleasures, or experiences would make us happy for
longer than they did? We have all made these mistakes, and yet
God waits for us, like a patient father.

Throughout the Bible we read powerful stories imbued with relentless invitations to turn back to God. Most of us have not abandoned him altogether, but we have abandoned him in one area of our lives. In what area of your life have you abandoned God? And why? Does some area of your life seem hopeless? Have you tried time and time again to turn back to him in that area and failed? Are you ashamed of that aspect of your life? Or is there something else in your past that is holding you back?

Augustine and so many of the saints are great beacons of hope for ordinary people like you and me. I look at Augustine and draw hope and strength from his story. I think to myself, "If he can turn it all around, surely God will work with me to turn my life around."

Yes, there may have been times in our lives when we tried with all our might to overcome a self-destructive habit and failed. Maybe we weren't ready, our hearts weren't really in it, or it just wasn't time.

Today is a new day, and every moment is a chance to turn it all around. Imagine that moment when Augustine finally surrendered. Weary of the world's broken promises, empty in his heart and in his soul, he finally turned to God. In that moment Augustine turned his whole life around. He probably didn't recognize how significant it was, and he couldn't have done it without God's help, but that was an amazing moment.

We all have moments like that in our lives—perhaps not as dramatic as Augustine's, but we all have turning points. Do you need one now? This might be the beginning of a new season of grace in your life. I hope it is. I pray it is. And somehow, somewhere, Augustine is hoping and praying for you too. He has experienced the discouragement and emptiness of the world and he has experienced God's incredible love, and he longs for you to experience it too, now more than ever before.

. . . .

LOVING FATHER,
Help us to know deep in our hearts that you are ready to remove today whatever obstacles we have placed between ourselves and you in the past. Open our hearts, minds, and souls to see the future you have imagined for us, and give us the courage to embrace your plans even when we feel inadequate and insecure. Amen.

2. WALTER:

An Overwhelming Love

. . . .

Have you ever allowed yourself to
rest in God's love?

GOD LOVES YOU. This statement is considered cliché and trite by the culture at large, and yet it is one of the greatest truths of the human experience. I am not sure what that says about us or about a society that belittles such profound truths.

We all have different experiences of God and his love, and in each personal experience there are meanings and mysteries that unfold throughout our lives.

I have always believed that God loves me. I'm not sure why. I don't remember anyone telling me this when I was a child, but for as long as I can remember I have believed it. Some people say that our experiences with our biological fathers have an impact on the way we see God. My own father was a good man and I grew up in his love and care, so perhaps that has something to do with it.

But if I had any doubts about God's love for me, they were quickly banished when my first child, Walter Patrick, named after his paternal and maternal great-grandfathers, was born. Those first weeks following his birth were an incredibly powerful spiritual time for me. I had this awe. I remember thinking, over and over again, "If I can love my son this much, and I am weak and broken, flawed and limited, imagine how much God loves us." My imperfect love provided profound insight into God's love.

Have you ever allowed yourself to rest in God's love? During those weeks following Walter's birth, I would go to my prayer time and I would just sit there and bathe in God's love. Letting go and allowing ourselves to rest in God's love is perhaps what Jesus had in mind when he said, "Come to me all you who are weary and carrying heavy burdens, and I will give you rest" (Matthew 11:28).

Try it today. Find a quiet place and just sit with God. Close your eyes. Take a few deep breaths. Breathe out all the stress and anxiety of your life. Breathe in God's life-giving oxygen. Think about the times in your life when you have loved someone deeply. Reflect on how intense your love for that person was despite your many limitations. Now consider the mystery of God's love, infinite and perfect. Try to imagine it, even though we are incapable of fully comprehending it. Once you have pondered the mystery for a few moments, ask God to let you just rest in his love.

Some of us are drawn into relationship with God early in life, others at the end of life, and some along the way. This is another of life's mysteries. Saint Walter of Serviliano was born in Rome and was fascinated with the study of God as a youth. He later became a Benedictine monk and went on to found a monastery in Italy.

Were you drawn into relationship with God early or later in

your life? Are you feeling called to a deeper connection with him right now? Perhaps this is a special moment of grace for you.

So, wherever you are today, I invite you to open yourself to God a little more by asking him to show you the power of his love. "Ask, and it will be given you; seek, and you will find; knock, and the door will be opened for you. For everyone who asks receives, and everyone who searches finds, and for everyone who knocks, the door will be opened" (Matthew 7:7–8).

· · · · · · · · · · · · · · · · · ·

FATHER OF ALL CREATION,
Show us the power of your love in new and special ways.
Open our hearts and minds to receive your love in all the
ways you want to share it with us. And allow your love
to flow through us to others, so that by knowing us they
might come to know you and your love a little more.
Amen.

3. IRENAEUS:

Fully Alive

. . . .

When was the last time you felt fully alive?

"THE GLORY OF GOD is man fully alive." Some words and ideas are so powerful that they change you even as you read them. This quote, which is attributed to Saint Irenaeus, had that effect on me the first time I read it when I was fifteen.

Religion and God are often accused of trying to limit people, when in reality they seek to bring the very best out of us. "Out of us" because God has already placed within us a self that is good. God and religion are often accused of trying to impose things upon people, but the reality is quite the opposite. God yearns for a dynamic relationship with each of his children, and through that relationship he seeks to draw out the-very-best-version-of-ourselves.

God is interested not only in our spiritual activities, but in every aspect of our lives. He is interested not only in our spiritual self, but in our whole self: physical, emotional, intellectual, and spiritual.

One of the reasons Irenaeus' quote struck me so powerfully when I first heard it is because it could just as plausibly have been written yesterday or by a bishop in the second century. One of the reasons it continues to fascinate me and resonate with me is because language has a tendency to invite and unite or to alienate and divide. Irenaeus' words are a beautiful invitation.

God doesn't stand down the road and call to us to catch up. He meets us where we are and leads us step-by-step to who he is calling us to become.

Jesus was constantly meeting people where they were, both physically and spiritually. He went to the people, met them in their hunger, blindness, homelessness, and sickness. The ailments Jesus attended to all have physical and spiritual manifestations. Sometimes we are physically hungry and sometimes we are spiritually hungry. Some people are physically homeless; others are spiritually homeless. Physical blindness is relatively uncommon, but we all suffer from spiritual blindness. And, of course, we all suffer from a variety of both physical and spiritual sicknesses throughout our lives.

The physical manifestations of each of these ailments are almost impossible to ignore, while the spiritual manifestations often require great awareness to uncover. This is one of life's mysteries. It is so easy to overlook what matters most.

"The glory of God is man fully alive" is an invitation to live life to the fullest and echoes Jesus' words, "I have come so that you may have life and have it to the fullest" (John 10:10).

Where does this life come from? How can we live life to the fullest? Only because God has placed his life within us, and that life is precious. When we waste time, we abuse that precious gift. When we avoid what we clearly know we should be doing, we are suppressing some aspect of God's life within us. Jesus tells us, "The kingdom of God is within you" (Luke 17:21), and I assume God is in his kingdom.

Man fully alive. Woman fully alive. You fully alive. What a beautiful idea. Imagine how life would be if you were thriving physically, emotionally, intellectually, and spiritually.

Are you fully alive? Are you living life to the fullest? What obstacles are preventing you from being fully alive and living life to the fullest? Do you pretend you don't know what they are? Do you believe those obstacles can be overcome? What would need to change for you to be fully alive?

The teachings of Jesus are constantly inviting us to experience life more fully. The saints are friends who remind us of that invitation and encourage us by their example to embrace life more fully. And in every place and every time, their example has always been a much more powerful teacher than speeches and books.

. . . .

FATHER OF ALL LIFE,
Teach us how to live life to the fullest. Give us the
courage to choose the-best-version-of-ourselves in
each and every moment of our days. And allow our
friendship and example to lead others to experience
what it means to be fully alive.
Amen.

4. BENEDICT:
Life-Giving Daily Routines

· · · · · · · · · · · · · · · · · · ·

Do your daily routines reinvigorate you?

FEW THINGS bring us happiness like deeply rooted daily routines. There is something about healthy routines and rituals that leads the human person to flourish.

This is something I have always struggled with. Creating strong routines around sleep, prayer, work, diet, exercise, and communion with friends and family is not something that comes easily to me. Perhaps it doesn't come easily to anyone. For a long time I blamed this on my life on the road, with all its irregularities. But while I admit that travel presents unique challenges to these life-giving routines, as I have grown older I have come to realize that what I need is more effort and fewer excuses.

The message of how important daily routines are has been delivered to me very powerfully on a number of occasions throughout my life. Four stand out as particularly important. The first was when I began to develop a daily routine of prayer as a teenager. Stopping by church for ten minutes each day powerfully focused my days and anchored them in what matters most.

The second was after a few years on the road had made me sick and tired. Retreating to the mountains of Austria, I discovered again how important ordinary and simple daily routines really are for both our health and holiness. I emerged from that experience and wrote *The Rhythm of Life*, which is a constant reminder to me of how important it is to maintain a healthy rhythm and yet how easy it is to lose that rhythm. But the deeper lesson was how easy it is to lose that rhythm doing good things and pursuing too many great opportunities.

The third time was during the research that gave birth to *The Four Signs of a Dynamic Catholic*. This research would ultimately form the foundation of the work Dynamic Catholic is doing. The first sign is a daily routine of prayer, and the power it has in calming and directing millions of people's lives is both obvious and astounding.

Finally, my fourth encounter with the power of daily routines was during a visit to Montecassino, a monastery in the mountains of southern Italy founded by Saint Benedict. In preparation for my visit, I had delved deeply into the life and writings of Benedict. This led me quickly to his masterwork, *The Rule of Saint Benedict*, which became the foundational document for thousands of religious communities from the Middle Ages to modern times. This book is a way of life laid out in seventy-three short chapters containing spiritual insights about how to live a Christ-centered life. It also contains practical and administrative guidance for monks and for the whole community regarding how to run a monastery.

The central precept of the work is the maxim *ora et labora,* which is Latin for *pray and work*. The monks devote eight hours each day to prayer, eight to work, and eight to sleep. These life-giving routines and rituals create a powerful rhythm in their lives.

Do you have powerful routines and rhythms that ground the days of your life in health, happiness, and holiness? I mention all three because I believe they are very strongly connected.

My whole life I have been fascinated with men and women who have been successful in any arena of human excellence. I have studied their lives and it always becomes quickly apparent that they each have their own "rule of life." They each have strong daily rituals and routines that allow their genius to flow and flourish. It's a powerful lesson—and even as I sit here writing, I know it is a lesson I need to learn again.

These days this lesson is ever present in the lives of my children. They thrive on routine. Disrupt that routine or take it away altogether and they are lost. When children's routines are disrupted they often misbehave, and it is easy to focus on this. But what they are really saying to us is that they are lost, that we have pulled the foundation of their days and weeks out from under them, and now they are confused and disoriented.

Saint Benedict understood the power of daily routines and rituals, and God collaborated with him to drive this wisdom deep into the life of the Church.

Jesus reminds us over and over again that we are all children, and without deeply rooted life-giving daily routines we become disoriented and lose sight of what matters most. Every aspect of Jesus' teachings encourages us to recognize the few things that are really important and to give those things priority in our lives.

. . . .

LOVING FATHER,
The tides come in and go out to a rhythm,
our hearts pump blood through our bodies to a
rhythm, and the sun rises and sets to a rhythm. Help
me to recognize the genius of rhythm in all you
created and to establish that rhythm in the days of my
life by celebrating strong daily routines and rituals.
Amen.

5. TERESA OF ÁVILA:
The First Routine

. . . .

Have you ever been taught how to pray?

MANY OF THE MOST amazing women in history are Catholic saints. Teresa of Ávila is just one example. She lived in the sixteenth century in a cloistered monastery, yet her influence throughout the world is so far reaching that it is impossible to measure. She was a Carmelite nun, an author, a reformer, and a mystic.

A mystic is a person who strives to become completely united with God through prayer and self-surrender. He or she often has mystical experiences, which could include having visions or hearing the voice of God. These experiences are thought of by most people as extraordinary, though many mystics have considered them to be a natural consequence of consistently opening ourselves to God.

Teresa of Ávila was one of the greatest mystics ever to live, and yet she was incredibly practical. It is an easy mistake to think of mystics as otherworldly or as living with their heads in the clouds—and while Teresa had astounding mystical experiences, she remained very aware of this life and this world and the struggles that ordinary people face.

She wrote about themes such as comfort and worry, how these things affect us, and how to deal with them. On the subject of comfort she wrote, "Our body has this defect that, the more it is provided care and comforts, the more needs and desires it finds."

When I was growing up, we didn't have air-conditioning or heating in our home or at school. Some days we were hot and some days we were cold, but we got along just fine. Today I have become so accustomed to these comforts that it seems like I cannot live without them.

More comfort is available to us than at any other time in history, and yet still we crave more. Teresa had this awareness five hundred years ago—three hundred years before indoor plumbing and electricity were invented.

We know Teresa suffered significant cruelty at the hands of other people. Many were jealous of her gifts and despised her out of envy. Others opposed her work to reform the Carmelite monastery out of self-interest or laziness. And even though she had this astounding relationship with God, it is clear that she struggled with worry.

When she died, an old handmade bookmark was found in her prayer book, which she used to take everywhere with her. On the bookmark Teresa had written, "Let nothing disturb you. Let nothing make you afraid. All things are passing. God alone never changes. Patience gains all things. If you have God you will want for nothing. God alone suffices."

Someone who doesn't struggle with worry wouldn't write something like that. Someone who hadn't wrestled with fear wouldn't keep those words so intimately close at all times.

Teresa of Ávila's astounding spiritual awareness combined with her attention to the practical things of life have fascinated me ever since she came into my life about thirty years ago. She taught me how to pray. By my mid-teens I knew of course how to say the Our Father and Hail Mary. I knew many prayers, but nobody had ever taught me to pray with my heart. Nobody had ever taught me to speak to God as a friend. Teresa of Ávila taught me how to have a conversation with God as if he were sitting across from me.

This type of intimate prayer is commonly referred to as mental prayer. Teresa encouraged me through her writings never to go to prayer without a spiritual book. She taught me to talk to God as I would a friend, beginning by sharing what is happening in my day or something that is on my mind. She taught me that distractions are an inevitable part of prayer. She taught me to return to my prayerful conversation with God the moment I realize I have become distracted. She taught me to turn to the spiritual book I have brought with me to prayer if I run out of things to discuss with God or if I find myself becoming distracted. She taught me to read a few paragraphs until something I'm reading sparks a new conversation with God.

Teresa of Ávila taught me how to pray. And she taught me that this type of prayer is a powerful form of contemplation. She taught me how to pray through her own experiences and writings, and I will be forever grateful.

Nothing will change a person's life like really learning how to pray. It is one of life's most powerful lessons. And yet, astonishingly, we don't teach people how to talk to God. We don't teach them to pray with their hearts in a deeply personal way. It is one of the areas of singular importance where we have fallen short as a Church.

Teaching people to pray is central to our mission as Christians. Everything good that we long for will be the fruit of prayer. Any worthwhile hope that we have for ourselves, our children, our families, the Church, and the world will be the result of a chain reaction set off by prayer. Prayer sets in motion a domino effect of goodness.

Without prayer, there is nothing.

This is an incredibly turbulent time in the Church, and people often ask me how we can forge a path forward as people of God. The only way forward is forward. What I mean to say is that we need to stop talking about it and start acting upon it, not with policies and procedures (though these certainly have their place), but by creating one holy moment at a time. That is how we create a path forward. And how will we summon the grace and courage necessary to create these holy moments? With prayer. All worthwhile action begins with prayer.

As a young man I was certain of so many things. The older I get, the less I am sure about, but I am absolutely certain of this when it comes to the future of the Catholic Church: If we do not teach people to pray, nothing will change. It is time for us to become a spiritual people again.

Whether they were young or old, educated or uneducated, rich or poor, healthy or sick, the saints all had one thing in common: Prayer had a central place in their lives. They had amazing friendships with God because they were men and women of prayer.

If you do nothing else with your life, develop an amazing friendship with God. Become a man or woman of prayer. This friendship will change the way you see yourself and the world. It will rearrange your priorities, as love always does. It will give you clarity and a joy that nobody can take from you.

We learn to live deeply by praying deeply. Find that place within you where you can connect with God, and start to spend time in that place every day. Find that place within you where you can discover more and more about the-best-version-of-yourself. Make your prayer time a sacred item on your schedule. Make it nonnegotiable.

Strong daily routines are life-giving, and prayer is the first of them.

. . . .

FATHER,
Thank you for all the ways you bless me, those I am aware of and all those I am still oblivious to. The Scriptures show me that from the beginning you have desired friendship with humanity. Help me to know and believe that just as you yearned for friendship with Adam and Eve; Abraham, Moses, and Noah; Ruth, Esther, Rachel, and Mary; you desire a powerful friendship with me. Give me the wisdom to make prayer a priority in my life so together we can foster a beautiful friendship.
Amen.

6. IGNATIUS:
Emotional Intelligence

. . . .

Are you an emotionally intelligent person?

IF WE REALLY want to understand what is happening in the world around us, we first need to explore what is happening within us.

I first met Ignatius of Loyola at Georgetown University during my third visit to the United States. Until then, I had heard his name in passing, but had never delved into his life and work. I had been invited there to speak by a group of Jesuits, and listening to their stories over dinner piqued my interest and I began to read Ignatius' *Spiritual Exercises*.

Two days later I was in New York for what would become one of the most important publishing meetings of my life. Sitting at breakfast overlooking Central Park, I was reading Ignatius when John F. Kennedy Jr. sat down at the table next to me. We were both alone and he asked me what I was reading. I could tell he was surprised and curious. We spoke for a few minutes and then I left for my meeting. The whole world was at his feet, but four years later he was dead at the age of thirty-eight.

The thing that struck me almost immediately about Ignatius' writings was how attuned they are to our humanity. Confined to his bed for months as he recovered from his battle injuries, he was forced to look at who he was as a man and the choices he had made. Over the course of those long weeks and months of recovery he measured his life and concluded that he was falling short of his God-given potential. He also reached the conclusion that he was being called to something more, though he had no idea what.

For many that would be enough, but Ignatius went further. He explored why he had made the choices he had made, and what his motives were for doing the things he had chosen to do. This led to a whole new level of awareness, and it is this ever-expanding awareness that became one of the enduring gifts of the *Spiritual Exercises*.

Over the past several years it has become popular to speak about the concept of emotional intelligence (EQ), in large part because it is disappearing from our culture at an alarming rate. So much of modern culture promotes a numbing unconsciousness rather than the vibrant consciousness that God wants us to live in each moment.

EQ is an awareness of what is happening within us and what the people around us are experiencing. It could be something as simple as realizing that your mood is a little off, perhaps because you didn't get enough sleep, and as a result you are more impatient than usual. Another simple example is you are having dinner with others and you notice someone's glass is empty, so you offer her another drink. Emotional intelligence is not only an awareness of what is happening within us and around us, it is ultimately an awareness of what is happening within the people around us. It is also an awareness of how what we do and say affects other people.

Do you notice when someone is happier or sadder than usual? There are some people we see every day. Can you tell if their spirits seem lighter or heavier than usual?

I believe Saint Ignatius is the father of emotional intelligence. He was a genius; we still have not fully realized his gift to humanity. Some people have unpacked it for themselves, but we have much work to do in unpacking it for those who are not called to study it intensely.

As I first read the *Spiritual Exercises* I was struck by the high EQ factor in the content. Lying in his bed, Ignatius got in touch with his emotional self in a way most people never do. As a result, he was able to recognize the Holy Spirit moving within him in very subtle ways. He discovered that one of the many ways God speaks to us is through our moods and emotions.

Ignatius left behind an incredible multifaceted legacy, but the crown jewel of that legacy is the *Spiritual Exercises*. My friendship with Ignatius spans more than two decades now. For the first five or six years I did my annual retreat at different Ignatian retreat centers with an Ignatian spiritual director. He helped me to delve deeper into the *Spiritual Exercises*.

I made one of my retreats at a center in Wernersville, Pennsylvania. At the time I was reading *He Leadeth Me*, by Walter Ciszek. In it Ciszek explains the spirituality that kept him alive, grateful, and focused on serving others rather than dying of self-pity during his twenty years as a prisoner in Russia. His crime: being a Catholic priest. At the beginning of the retreat, my spiritual director asked me, "What are you planning to read during your retreat this year?" I told him and he smiled. "Did you know Father Ciszek is buried here on the retreat center grounds?" I didn't. It was one of those moments that send shivers up your spine. The saints are always around us. The next day I walked over to his grave site and spent some time there in prayer and reflection.

The spirituality of Saint Ignatius of Loyola transformed Walter Ciszek's life and inspired him to go to Russia as a missionary priest. Ciszek may soon be declared a saint, but regardless, he was a man who filled his life with holy moments. I wonder how many more holy men and women have been touched, inspired, encouraged by Saint Ignatius of Loyola and his pioneering spiritual work. Thousands? Millions? We will never know. What we do know is that holiness is contagious. The good we do never dies. It lives on forever—in other people, in other places, and in other times.

· · · · · · · · · · · · · · · · · ·

FATHER,
Teach me to listen deeply to what is happening within me and to discern what you are saying to me through my hopes and dreams, fears and failures, joy and sadness. Give me a piercing awareness of what is happening within me and around me, so that I can love you more, love others to the best of my ability, and love myself as you love me.
Amen.

7. FRANCIS OF ASSISI:
Dissatisfied

· · · · · · · · · · · · · · · · · ·

What are you dissatisfied with at this time in your life?

WE ARE ALL writing the story of our lives. Are you satisfied with the story you are writing with your life?

Francis of Assisi is the most popular saint in the world today, largely because of his appeal to non-Catholics and even non-Christians. Eight hundred years after his death people are just as fascinated with him as they were during his lifetime.

As a young man Francis became profoundly dissatisfied with his life. He had spent his youth being the life of the party, but that began to leave him feeling empty. This emptiness led him to a belief that there simply must be more to life.

These are feelings we have all experienced, but how we respond to them makes all the difference. Francis followed the Spirit and rebelled in a truly wild and wonderful way. By allowing the Spirit to guide him, he wrote a beautiful story with his life.

Are you dissatisfied with your life? Francis' story teaches us that we should listen to that dissatisfaction, find out what is causing it, and then respond rather than reacting. Too often we react to our dissatisfaction impulsively, but there is a difference between reacting and responding. Our tendency is to react to the dissatisfaction in our lives—by taking a last-minute vacation, going shopping, eating or working more, and so on. We all have our favorite ways of distracting ourselves from looking at the real questions of our lives. As we grow spiritually our awareness increases, and as we grow in awareness we learn to respond rather than react.

Francis heard God saying to him, "Rebuild my Church." He reacted by literally rebuilding a dilapidated church. That was his reaction. But once he had finished rebuilding the church near his home, he continued to hear God saying to him, "Francis, rebuild my Church." This led him to the awareness that God was inviting him to rebuild the Church spiritually. He dedicated the rest of his life to spiritual renewal. That was his response.

The difference between reaction and response is often a period of investigation, however brief, between something that happens and our respone to it. During that period of investigation, we ask ourselves a series of questions designed to help us understand what is really happening within us and around us.

A common example might be dissatisfaction at work. You might react and think, "I need to find a new job." Now, it may be that God is calling you to a new role and using your feelings of dissatisfaction to lead you there. But he may be trying to communicate to you any number of other things. You may be dissatisfied at work because you are not working as hard as you need to. This may be because you have lost focus, or it may be because you have a sick child or parent you are taking care of at home. You may be dissatisfied because the people you work with are petty and difficult. They may be petty and difficult because they are suffering in some way, and God may be inviting you to love them out of their pettiness. You may be dissatisfied at work because you have lost sight of the people you serve with your work and how it improves their lives. Your dissatisfaction may be caused by something large or small, and to some extent it doesn't matter what the cause is. What matters is how you respond to that dissatisfaction.

God is allowing that dissatisfaction for a reason. Listen to it. What area of your life are you dissatisfied with? How is God inviting you to a new and better life? How is he inviting you to become a-better-version-of-yourself through this situation?

Again, our instinct is to react, and often we overreact. Our dissatisfaction may not be calling us to go somewhere new and do something different. It may be inviting us to go deeper into what we are doing right now.

The other option is to ignore our dissatisfaction, pretend that all is well when it isn't. If we choose this path our dissatisfaction will grow in an attempt to get our attention.

Francis was dissatisfied. God used his dissatisfaction to invite him to go wild in a wonderful way by rebelling against the norms and expectations society had placed on him and his life. He surprised people by abandoning himself to God and he wrote an incredible story with his life.

In some ways his story could not be more different than that of Teresa of Ávila or Ignatius of Loyola, but in other ways their stories are remarkably similar. They each allowed themselves to be led by the Holy Spirit, they were dedicated to living a life of prayer, they valued Jesus' opinion more than anyone else's, and they were committed to creating holy moments.

During Mass we pray, "You renew the Church in every age by raising up men and women outstanding in holiness, living witnesses of your love. They inspire us by their heroic lives, and help us by their constant prayers." God raised up Francis, Irenaeus, Augustine, Teresa, and Ignatius to renew the Church. They are living witnesses of God's love, and their stories captivate our imaginations and inspire us still today. Each in their own way, in their own place and time, wrote a story with their life, and now it is your turn.

Some of us may be thinking, "It's too late. I'm too old. Most of my life is over." Well, there are many different types of stories. Perhaps yours is one of redemption from regret and hopelessness. Maybe your story will have a surprise ending or an unexpected twist.

It's time to pay attention to the story you are writing with your life. Great stories move people. If yours isn't inspiring you, then it probably isn't going to move anyone else. It's time to live a life that intrigues people, one that challenges people to rethink their own lives. It's time to live a life that fascinates people, a life that moves people.

Does that seem grandiose and impossible? It isn't. We all carry the seeds of greatness within us. Sometimes that greatness manifests in extraordinary things, but most of the time the greatness of God manifests in us through ordinary things done with great love.

There are so many small, ordinary things you and I can do each day to remind people that the goodness and generosity, thoughtfulness and compassion that make the human spirit great are alive and well. Life is always presenting a steady stream of these opportunities to collaborate with God and create holy moments. Each is a chance to let people know that somebody cares, sometimes with a small gesture and sometimes in more significant ways. That is what the saints did. They collaborated with God and unleashed goodness, generosity, thoughtfulness, and compassion wherever they went. You can do that too.

The human spirit may be asleep, but it is not dead. Let's awaken the greatness of the human spirit, starting with you and me. Wake your spirit. Wake up spiritually and start to live life on a whole new level.

. . . .

LORD,

Thank you for the vast array of feelings and emotions that you allow me to experience. Teach me to listen to the dissatisfaction in my life and discover what you are saying to me through it. Then give me the courage and boldness to do something about it.

Amen.

8. THOMAS MORE:
The Gentle Voice Within

· · · · · · · · · · · · · · · · · ·

When was the last time you paused to listen to your conscience before making a decision?

SOMETIMES THE BEST way to reflect upon the story of our lives is to ponder death. Life is wonderful but short. The saints meditated on death so that they wouldn't take a moment of this precious life for granted. Life has a tendency to slip through our hands like water, unless we live each day, each hour, each moment with great consciousness. The saints nurtured this conscious awareness with daily prayer.

Saint Thomas More first crossed my path in high school. I was working as a stage hand for the school play, *A Man for All Seasons*. My brother Andrew had been cast in the role of Cromwell. It began with the cast and crew sitting around reading the script. I'd never met a man like Thomas. Some nights I would practice reading lines with my brother so he could master his part. And once the set was built there were dozens of rehearsals. The play and its message were driven deep into my heart, mind, and soul.

Thomas was executed on July 6, 1535, in London for re-fusing to recognize the Act of Supremacy and sign the Act of Succession. The former made King Henry VIII the head of the Church of England and the latter required all those asked to take an oath that recognized Anne Boleyn as the king's lawful wife and their children as legitimate heirs to the throne.

Thomas More was widely regarded as a man of impeccable character and meticulous honesty. People trusted his judgment, and his refusal to sign sent a message to the people of England. He didn't speak out against the acts; he simply refused to sign or say anything at all. But one honest man's silence is louder than all the words of ten thousand dishonest men.

The king accused Thomas of treason and the punishment was death. Thomas explained to his family that he could not in good conscience sign the document because he did not believe it to be true or right. He was willing to die rather than betray God, his country, his conscience, and the-very-best-version-of-himself.

When was the last time you refused to do something because your conscience made it clear that it was wrong? When was the last time you paused to listen to your conscience before making a decision? Have you ever regretted following your conscience?

When we ignore our conscience, we betray ourselves, others, and God.

There is a curious lightness of being that comes with a clear conscience. My grandfather used to say we sleep better with a clear conscience. A clear conscience is profound, simple, com-plex, mysterious, and liberating all at the same time. It is both simple and complex because we have a responsibility to devel-op and form our conscience, and to align it with the truth in all things. Listening to our conscience is relatively easy once we begin to consistently make the effort. Continually developing our conscience is quite difficult and complex. Knowing when to let go of things you once thought were true in favor of greater truths is psychologically and spiritually challenging. It requires courage and grace.

We live in a world where we are constantly told, "Do whatever you feel like doing," and that message is reinforced with the idea that doing what you want and getting what you want will make you happy. The concept of conscience seems long forgotten in such a world. A sense of right and wrong has been lost, washed away by a tidal wave of relativism.

And yet, deep within you there is a gentle voice, the voice of your conscience. It is the-best-version-of-yourself whispering to you in the moments of your day. When we listen to it, we experience a joy and lightness; when we ignore it, our soul aches and we experience a profound feeling of being weighed down.

It's strange how we prefer new ideas that don't bear fruit to ancient ideas that bear fruit every time. Why are we so ready to abandon the tried-and-true? There is beauty in our faith. It is old, yes—ancient, in fact—but it still bears incredible fruit when it is lived with passion and purpose. And maybe a clear conscience does help us sleep better.

History has weighed the life of Sir Thomas More and named him a saint. All lives are measured in the end—it serves us well to remember that—and it is men and women like Thomas More who inspire us to live courageously even in the face of great opposition. This is perhaps when and where the saints are most helpful to us, when times are tough. They demonstrate how to behave in the face of adversity, injustice, and even cruelty. And of course, they learned how to courageously encounter adversity by patiently reflecting on the way Jesus lived his life.

The saints teach us to live boldly by listening to that gentle voice within. Are you living the one short life you have been given with passion and purpose?

. . . .

FATHER,
Thank you for my one short life. Inspire me in some small way each day to live with grace and courage, compassion and generosity, by listening to the gentle voice that you have placed within me.
Amen.

9. JOHN:

Friendship

. . . .

Do you allow people to really get to know you?

I LISTEN TO my children pray at night, and I realize how far I am from the heart of God. "What would you like to say to Jesus tonight?" I ask them, and they talk to him as if he were there in the room with them, excited to hear the tiniest details of their day, a friend like no other.

If you had to describe Jesus to a person who had never heard of him, how would you do it? On one level this might seem like a very difficult task, but on another level, it is really quite simple. Christianity is spread by telling Jesus' story. The beautiful thing about someone who has never heard about Jesus is that they have not been inoculated against Christianity and they don't carry with them all the bias and prejudice that surrounds Jesus and Christianity in our society today. The person who has never heard about Jesus would be absolutely fascinated with his story, because even if it were just a story, it would be amazing. When you consider that it actually happened, it becomes even more intriguing, powerful, and life-altering.

One of our biggest problems as Christians is that we have become too familiar with the story of Jesus. They say familiarity breeds contempt. Let's consider the meaning of that phrase for a moment. It means that as our knowledge and association with someone or something grows, our respect for that person or thing diminishes.

This is also one of the biggest problems we have in our relationships with the saints. We think we know them. We may know when they lived or some other cursory facts about their lives, but not the deep and abiding soul-changing habits that made them who they are. And not the unique message they have for each of us as we really get to know them.

This was also the great challenge of this book: how to write about the saints in a way that is fresh and will pierce through the casual assumptions we have about them; how to give you a broad understanding of what binds them together, and yet personally *introduce* you to the ones who are most important to you in your journey right now.

Two of my favorite saints are John the Baptist and John the Apostle. They both had very special relationships with Jesus, yet those relationships could not have been more different.

John the Baptist first met Jesus when they were both unborn children in their mothers' wombs. There is no record of them meeting again until John baptized Jesus in the river Jordan, though it seems likely that they spent time together as children, given the lengths Mary went to in order to visit John's mother during her pregnancy. Nonetheless, when John encountered Jesus the day of his baptism, familiarity or not, there was the complete opposite of contempt. John held Jesus not only in great respect, but with reverence.

What I love about John the Baptist is his distance from Jesus.

He had a job to do and he got it done. He wasn't coming to Jesus asking, "How am I doing?" He knew what he needed to do, and he took care of it.

John the Apostle had the opposite relationship in many respects. He was tremendously close to Jesus and spent three years at his side. He had the courage to stand at the foot of the cross—the only man among a group of brave women. And he is referred to six times in the Gospel as the disciple Jesus loved.

Would you like to have a special relationship with Jesus? I would. Not to be different from or better than anyone else, but just to have something that is unique between me and God. I suppose it is a very natural and normal desire for any Christian. The hardest part seems to be getting out of the way, pushing aside our ego and expectations, and letting it unfold rather than trying to force it. Come to think of it, that seems to be the hardest part of life and relationships in general.

How would you describe your relationship with Jesus? For the saints everything was about him. They placed Jesus at the center of their lives by placing him at the center of everything they did. They discovered the-best-version-of-themselves in and through Jesus.

How is your relationship with Jesus? Or perhaps it would help to consider some other questions. How do you wish to be known? What do you want your reputation to be? How do you want to be remembered? Would you like to be remembered for your accomplishments or for your character? Would you like to be remembered for what you did or who you were? Do you want to be remembered as a worldly person or a spiritual person? Do you hope to be thought of as a disciple of Jesus?

We remember the saints because they had unique and intimate relationships with Jesus. Some might say they had extraordinary relationships with him, but I believe that God wants us all to have that kind of relationship with his son. God wants that kind of relationship to be ordinary and natural, carefree and unaffected, just like the way my children speak to Jesus before they go to bed.

Jesus is your friend, and great friends take a genuine interest in each other. They are loyal and honest. They focus on giving, not taking. They build each other up with encouragement. Great friends are empathetic. They are good listeners, and they help us to see the humorous side of life.

If you could choose anyone in history to teach you about friendship, whom would you choose?

It is through our relationship with Jesus that we learn how to be a good friend to others. He teaches us what it means to truly be a friend. He teaches us how to relate to others with compassion and understanding. He teaches us when to speak and when to listen.

Think about all the gods people have worshipped throughout the ages, in different places and cultures and times. One of the astounding things that make the God of the Judeo-Christian tradition different is that he wants to be your friend. The saints recognized this. They didn't care if people noticed or remembered what they did. They didn't care about their reputation at all. They cared about their relationship with Jesus, and from that flowed all the goodness and genius they shared with the world.

Do you think John would rather be known as a saint, as an apostle, or as Jesus' friend?

"Seek first the kingdom of God" (Matthew 6:33), we read in the Scriptures. In real and practical terms, what does it mean to seek first the kingdom of God? It means to enter into a life-giving relationship with him and make that friendship a daily priority. It means to keep the main thing the main thing, and the main thing is your friendship with God.

The saints were God's friends on this earth. And now it's your turn.

. . . .

LORD,
Inspire me to care more about my friendship
with you than about my accomplishments in
this world. Help me to make our time together each
day a sacred and nonnegotiable touchstone of daily
life. Teach me how to be a good friend to others.
Amen.

10. MARTHA:
Our longing for belonging

. . . .

Are you part of a vibrant community?

WE ALL YEAR to belong to a loving community. Modern psychology has redefined this as a need to belong. Our longing for belonging is real, but it's also more than that.

We each have a God-given need to belong to a community based on love for one another, where we can each contribute according to our gifts and abilities, and where we can be seen and known for who we really are—warts and all, so to speak. This is what made the very first Christian communities unique and fascinating.

God created us with certain needs and he provides for the fulfillment of these needs. In his plan our need for loving community is first met by our family. But the selfishness of men and women often leads families into dysfunction, and God's vision for family is destroyed. God also desires to fulfill this need we have to belong through dynamic and loving Christian communities.

The parish of my childhood was Saint Martha's, in suburban Sydney, Australia. I was Baptized there, experienced First

Reconciliation and First Communion there, was Confirmed there, and participated in an amazing multigenerational youth group experience there. It was the Christian community that launched me into life and the ministry I have committed myself to for the past twenty-five years.

As I have traveled the world it has become very clear to me that the local parish is the heartbeat of the Church around the world. It is how and where more than a billion Catholics engage in Christian community, yet our modern parishes don't resemble the first Christian communities very much at all.

When I founded Dynamic Catholic, my original dream was to work out how to transform parishes into phenomenal life-giving Christian communities. But one of our first discoveries was that you simply cannot have a dynamic parish without world-class resources in essential areas. This realization delayed my original dream for a decade as we spent the first ten years at Dynamic Catholic creating the Catholic Moments series—ten essential programs that every parish uses every year, made available to every parish and every Catholic at little or no cost. Now as we venture into our second decade at Dynamic Catholic we are passionately working with communities across the United States to create dynamic parishes.

There are many aspects of any authentic Christian community, and the piece we learn from Saint Martha is hospitality. Hospitality was at the heart of the earliest Christian communities; it set the first Christians apart in an age when care, concern, and love for others was foreign to people. And it is one of the ways modern Catholics can differentiate themselves in the current society.

Saint Martha is most remembered for the day Jesus visited her home and her sister, Mary, sat at his feet rather than helping

Martha prepare the meal. Jesus said to her, "Martha, Martha, you are worried and distracted by many things; but only one thing is necessary" (Luke 10:41–42). What was he saying? What lesson is here for us? If we read the words literally, we could be led to believe Jesus was saying that preparing the meal was not necessary. Man does not live on bread alone; he also lives on the Word of God. But neither does man live in the Word of God alone, and so clearly someone has to prepare our meals.

The genius of the Gospels is that they speak to us all according to where we are at different times in our lives. I am a practical person, so I find it much easier to take action than to sit at Jesus' feet in prayer and listen. Like Martha, I am often worried and distracted by many things. My mind is constantly swirling with a thousand things that need to be done. So, Jesus' words convict me to do my part but to worry less, and not to be constantly distracted by action, but instead to pause for prayer so that my action springs forth from my relationship with God.

Martha was a fabulous host; she was also a woman of great faith who loved Jesus deeply and obviously had a very special relationship with him. There is a certain casual nature to each of Jesus' encounters with Martha and her siblings, Mary and Lazarus. No other family is singled out in the Gospels like this one. "Jesus loved Martha, and her sister Mary, and Lazarus" (Luke 11:5).

Martha displays one of the most astounding professions of faith in the Gospels after her brother's death. When Jesus arrives, days after Lazarus has died, she boldly says to him, "Lord, if you had been here, my brother would not have died. But I know that even now God will give you whatever you ask" (John 11:21–22).

Martha's great gift was hospitality, *but even our great gifts are not more important than sitting with the Lord.*

As with so many people in the Scriptures, the rest of Martha's life is lost to time. One tradition says that she, along with Mary, was one of the women who came to the tomb to anoint the body of Jesus after the crucifixion. A famous legend claims that Mary and Martha traveled to Provence in France, eventually ending up in Tarascon, where Martha tamed a dragon-like monster. Her remains are said to be in the crypt of the church there.

The truth is we don't know what happened to Martha after Jesus' death, Resurrection, and Ascension. What we do know is that she was one of his earliest followers and one of the first to pronounce him the Messiah. And we know that she must have been a pretty good cook and a wonderful housekeeper, and that hospitality was one of her core values—a value she no doubt spread among the early Christians.

There are so many lessons and invitations that arose from Martha's encounters with Jesus. Which one is stirring in you at this moment? Is Jesus inviting you to sit at his feet more regularly and listen to his voice in your life? Is he inviting you to rediscover the spirit of hospitality? Is he asking you to bring your worries to him and place them on the altar at Mass each Sunday to let him deal with them? Is he encouraging you not to put the distractions of this world ahead of what matters most? Or perhaps he is speaking to you in some other deeply personal way through this reflection on the life of Saint Martha.

One lesson I would like to encourage us all to take away here is that whatever saint your parish is named after, that saint wants to lead, teach, and inspire the people of your community in a special way. So many of us know little or nothing about the patron saint of our own parishes. Your first parish, last parish, and every parish in between has a patron saint that wants to teach you a powerful lesson.

As for belonging to a vibrant community, we each have a role in creating that reality. In the past I have raised two questions: (1) There are seventy million Catholics in America. If we multiplied your life by seventy million, what would the Church in America be like? (2) There are more than a billion Catholics around the world today. If they were all like you, what would the Church be like?

Now let's focus these questions locally for a moment. It seems to me that everyone wants to belong to a dynamic parish. Even the people who only come to church at Christmas want to come to a dynamic parish and have a dynamic experience. Is your parish dynamic? Many are not. But the question is, what are you and I going to do about it? How are you willing to participate and contribute to your parish to help it become more dynamic each year?

If every person in your parish were as engaged or disengaged as you, how dynamic would your parish be?

. . . .

LOVING FATHER,
Open my heart to the areas of my life that
need to change so that I can carry out the mission
you have imagined for my life. Inspire me to live the
Catholic faith in ways that are dynamic and engaging.
Show me how best to get involved in the life of my
parish. Make our community hungry for best practices
and continuous learning, and help us to realize that we
each have a role to play in making our parish a perfect
place for imperfect people trying to walk with you.
Amen.

11. VINCENT DE PAUL:
God Feeds Us to Feed Others

. . . .

Are your friends helping you become the-best-version-of-yourself?

THE SAINTS are always around us, and their lives are intertwined with each other's and with ours.

During my last couple of years of high school, the students would take turns visiting a homeless shelter in the seediest part of Sydney. The men were homeless primarily because of alcoholism. The place was called Matt Talbot's and was run by the St. Vincent de Paul Society. We would visit on Friday nights, serve the men their dinner, and then sit and talk to them. My introverted-self hated it.

But this is how Vincent de Paul, Frederic Ozanam, Rosalie Rendu, and Matt Talbot entered my life, and they have never been too far from me, each for their own reasons.

Vincent de Paul was a Catholic priest in France who was ordained in 1600 and dedicated his life to serving the poor. Known for his humility, compassion, and generosity, he was widely loved and admired by the people of his time.

Frederic Ozanam was a French scholar, journalist, and equal

rights advocate. While at university, he gathered with his fellow students each week to debate various topics. One week the conversation turned to the Catholic Church. Some began to argue that while the Church had once been a source of good, it no longer was.

One student issued the challenge that would forever change Frederic's life and the lives of millions of men and women around the world: "What is your Church doing now? What is she doing for the poor of Paris? Show us your works and we will believe you!" Frederic reflected on the angry student's words and could not find fault with what he had said. At that moment he decided a major theme of his life would be serving the poorest people in Paris. But he had no idea how to begin. He knew where to find the city's poor, but he didn't know how to approach them, what they needed most, or how best to help them.

His reading led him to be inspired by a priest who had lived in France two hundred years earlier, Vincent de Paul. Further reading led him to discover that one of Vincent's followers, Sister Rosalie Rendu, was currently serving the poor in the slums of Paris. Frederic approached Sister Rendu and asked her to help him and his fellow students develop a method to serve the poor that could easily be taught to more and more students over time. "Where are these fellow students?" she asked.

"They will come," he replied, though he wasn't sure they would.

Inspired by Frederic's appeal to them, the other students did come. Sister Rendu mentored them and helped them develop a method to serve the poor. This would become the method that the St. Vincent de Paul Society uses even to this day in dozens of countries around the world. It focuses on visiting the poor in their homes, assessing their needs, and discerning how the society can best help each person or family.

Frederic Ozanam ultimately founded the St. Vincent de Paul

Society. He did it out of humility and a deep sense of gratitude to both the man who inspired him to believe it was possible to effectively serve the poor, and the woman who mentored him and his friends in the practical realities of that work: Vincent de Paul and Sister Rosalie Rendu.

Matt Talbot was an Irish dock worker, and an alcoholic from the age of twelve. When he was twenty-eight, he pledged never to drink alcohol again, and he kept that pledge for the next forty years, until his death. He spent those forty years working hard, paying back his debts, giving everything he had to the poor, sleeping on nothing but a wooden plank, and praying for several hours a day.

After his death, Talbot became an icon of Ireland's temperance movement, and his story spread around the world. He is quoted as saying, "Never be too hard on the man who can't give up drink. It's as hard to give up the drink as it is to raise the dead to life again. But both are possible and even easy for Our Lord. We have only to depend on him." Today one of Dublin's bridges bears his name, as do many addiction clinics and homeless shelters around the world, from Warsaw to Nebraska to Sydney.

And that is how at seventeen years of age I found myself feeding the poor and talking to a group of homeless men on a Friday night. I didn't know it at the time, but I was being taught one of the most difficult yet essential lessons of the Christian life: We are called to have a relationship with the poor.

Do you have a relationship with the poor? If we want to have a personal relationship with God, we need to have a personal relationship with the poor.

The good we do is never lost; it never dies. The good we do lives on in other people, in other places, and in other times. Vincent de Paul, Frederic Ozanam, Sister Rosalie Rendu, and Matt Talbot all faced tremendous discouragement at times. It would have been so easy to give up, to retreat into a comfortable life. But they didn't. They pressed on, persevering in humble service, and the good they did lives on today.

One of the things that set the saints apart were their friends. Many of the saints had friends who were also saints. They befriended the saints of ages past through books, because they realized that in the lives of the saints they could find what today we call "best practices." In this way they studied what had worked for other saints. But the number of saints who had friends who also became saints is enormous. Some of them knew each other and worked together, others had friendships that consisted entirely of letters, some were siblings, and others, such as Frederic Ozanam and Sister Rosalie Rendu, crossed paths unexpectedly but providentially.

Holy moments set off a domino effect. The saints had friends who encouraged them to become the-best-version-of-themselves, grow in virtue, and live holy lives. Do you have a good group of people around you who encourage and challenge you to grow? Are you a good friend to others, encouraging them toward what is good?

Sooner or later we rise or fall to the level of our friendships.

· · · · · · · · · · · · · · · · · ·

LORD,
Thank you for all the opportunities you have given me to grow spiritually. Thank you for all the ways you provide for my physical, material, emotional, and spiritual needs. Help me to keep in mind that you feed me and build me up to send me out to do the same for others.
Amen.

12. HARRY:
With Your Whole Heart

. . . .

***When was the last time you did something
with your whole heart?***

IT'S GOOD to have heroes, but too often we expect too much of our heroes and too little of ourselves.

My grandfather Harry was one of my heroes. He grew up in the Great Depression, fought in World War II, and worked hard the rest of his life to support his family. He struggled his whole life with what today we would call post-traumatic stress disorder, and spent his retirement volunteering at the local St. Vincent de Paul center.

He was a quiet man, but you could tell there was real strength behind his quiet ways. I remember hanging around in his workshop as a child. He could fix anything. He always wanted to show me how to fix things, but I never was very interested. It wasn't my gift, though I did love watching him make and fix things.

Nobody will canonize him, but in his own way, in his own place, in his own time, he was a saint in the broader sense of the word. The saints—canonized and not—are all around us, all the time. None of them are perfect, but all of them are striving with all their hearts. When was the last time you did something with all your heart?

My grandfather was named after Saint Harold, who was martyred in England as a child. Little is known about him other than the fact that he was killed by an anti-Christian faction. Why did they choose to kill him? We don't know.

Why are we humans so cruel to each other? That is one of the great mysteries of the human experience. My grandfather witnessed so many forms of human cruelty, yet he chose to focus on the good in people and situations and went out of his way to do good for others every day. It was only as I got older and began to experience the world that I realized how good a man he was and that he became a hero to me.

The saints are there during life's great highs and celebrations, and they are there in those dark moments when life brings us low. They are never far away, and they always bring with them the lesson we need to make the onward journey. They may bring a lesson of humility when we feel on top of the world, or a lesson of persistence when we feel like we cannot go on.

We named our third child after my grandfather, Harold James. When little Harry was born, there was a new type of magic in the house as we brought him home to Walter and Isabel, their eyes opened wide as they discovered their little brother for the first time. Their awe and innocence as they took his tiny hands in theirs and the way they instantly loved him and were concerned for him was beautiful to witness. For weeks, in different ways, they would ask if he needed anything. They didn't know what he needed, but they knew he needed. And don't we all. We need. It's part of what it means to be human.

Harry is five now and already growing into a fine young man. He has incredible intuition and a great sense of caring for others. He is sensitive. He feels things deeply and he is also very attuned to other people's feelings. Once he decides to do something, he throws himself into it with his whole heart. Even when he roars like a lion, his whole little body trembles. I am excited to watch him grow as his life unfolds, and honored to be able to accompany him in some way along that path.

Everything is an opportunity to create holy moments, to grow in holiness, and to become a-better-version-of-ourselves. Parenting is an endless opportunity, but so is being a sibling. Earlier we spoke about Saint Benedict. His sister, Scholastica, is also a saint. This leads us to question ourselves in a very practical way: Am I helping my siblings become the-best-version-of-themselves? Do my words and actions encourage them to love God and create holy moments?

The saints are always swirling around us, coming in and out of our lives when we need them most, and pointing out every opportunity to create more holy moments. Being a parent, being a sibling, being a spouse, work and play, friendship and community, sickness and health . . . every moment is a chance to create one more holy moment. How will you collaborate with God to create your next holy moment? Is your heart in it? Is it a wholehearted collaboration?

. . . .

FATHER,
Empty my heart of all the useless attachments superficial desires, and selfish inclinations so that I can give my whole heart to loving you and the people who cross my path.
Amen.

13. JOHN VIANNEY:

Disoriented

· · · · · · · · · · · · · · · · · ·

*Are you open to the possibilities that
only God can see for you?*

GOD IS ALWAYS found in the present moment, but the present moment can seem brutal at times, and that brutality can make him seem very far away.

In my late teens I began to ask the big question: God, what do you want me to do with my life? I had always thought I would get married and have a family, but in asking the question I began to sense God's call upon my life. As a young man growing up in the era I did, that meant only one thing: priesthood. What other options were there? None. Young men who felt called to serve God and his people became priests, and so I began to explore this path.

John Vianney, known as the Curé of Ars, crossed my path around that time and has remained in my heart as one of my heroes ever since. Unable to keep up with his studies in the seminary, John Vianney scraped through to ordination only because of the intervention of a bishop attuned to the Holy Spirit who sensed in Vianney a special gift from God.

After ordination Vianney was sent to Ars, a village in rural France. It might as well have been the end of the world. That is certainly where they intended to send him, so he could do as little damage as possible. But over the next thirty years, Ars would become one of the most popular Catholic pilgrimage destinations in Europe. So many people traveled to see John Vianney that the government built a train line to carry passengers directly to Ars. Ten years after he died they ripped it up because it was no longer used.

People went to encounter the Curé of Ars—to see him, to hear him preach, and to go to confession. He sat in the confessional every day for ten, twelve, fourteen hours. He listened deeply to people and spoke to them with compassion, love, courage, and wisdom.

We all have questions we are grappling with, and we yearn for answers to those questions. Our hearts, minds, and souls are not satisfied with answers that are quoted at us by rote. We long for deeply personal answers to our deeply personal questions. John Vianney sat in that confessional day after day, year after year, listening to the challenges and heartaches people were grappling with, and dispensing deeply personal answers to their deeply personal questions. It was an extraordinary ministry of grace and mercy.

He inspired me and fanned the flame within me to become a priest. As the months passed, the call to serve God and his people grew stronger. I had been filled with an incredible joy and I wanted to share that joy with other people. In the weeks that followed this realization I made an appointment with the vocations director. I was surprised that it took several weeks to get an appointment, but when the time came we spoke for about forty-five minutes. When we were finished he suggested I come back a couple of weeks later to continue the process.

When I returned two weeks later, I immediately sensed that

something was off. The director spoke about football for about ten minutes and then without warning said, "Well, Matthew, I have spoken to the archbishop and we have decided that you are not a suitable candidate for the priesthood." My whole world began to spin and my ears started ringing.

"What does that mean?" I asked.

"We just don't think you are a suitable candidate."

"Yes, you said that, but what does that mean? What is it that prevents me from being a so-called suitable candidate? What attributes of a suitable candidate am I lacking?"

"Well, Matthew, I think it's probably better that we don't get into all of that." He then abruptly ended the meeting, and in an instant, I was walking down the street trying to make sense of what had just happened.

The present moment can be brutal, and God can seem very far away.

That was the first time the Church broke my heart. It would be the first of many, unfortunately. I was sad and disillusioned; I felt like my compass was broken. How had I gotten it so wrong? When you think you know the will of God and you surrender yourself to it, and then something prevents you from pursuing that path, you begin to doubt your ability to discern what God is calling you to, even in the smallest things.

Almost thirty years later I understand that God was at work in that moment of rejection, but it still hurts, even today. In that moment it was impossible for my young and inexperienced self to realize that God is constantly at work—that when men block God's way, he finds another way. Today, I can look back and see that God had not abandoned me; his hand was on my shoulder, guiding me and protecting me, and he had dreams for me that I could not even imagine. We see what is possible based on what has been done in the past, but God sees new possibilities.

Back then, there was no path for a layperson to do the work I have done for almost three decades. I didn't see the path then and I don't see the path forward now. I woke up each day, prayed, asked God to guide me, and did what I felt he was calling me to do—one day at a time.

We find vocation where our needs, talents, and desire to serve others collide with the world's insatiable need. And we don't have just one vocation in this life. Yes, we have a primary vocation, but we also have secondary vocations. There is no doubt in my mind that this work I have been doing all these years is a vocation, but not my primary vocation. My primary vocation is as a husband and father. And someday I hope to be a grandfather, and then I will be called to the vocation of being a grandparent. It is a secondary vocation—a path within the path—but how beautiful these other vocations can be.

We are surrounded by possibilities that only God can see. What is God calling you to now? Is he clarifying your primary vocation in your heart? Does he have some temporary or secondary vocation that he wants you to dedicate yourself to at this time in your life? The danger is that we are so attached to our own plans that we cannot even see his plan.

. . . .

LORD,
I am open to your possibilities. Please fill me with the wisdom, grace, and courage I need to step out of my self-imposed limitations and live in your possibilities.
Amen.

14. THOMAS:
We All Have Doubts

. . . .

Do your doubts unsettle you,
or do you see them as an invitation to grow?

FAITH AND DOUBT go hand in hand, and often, the greater the faith, the greater the doubt.

Our doubts can be a great antagonist in our faith story. This antagonist often draws us into a deeper experience of faith as long as we remain in pursuit of truth and don't begin to pursue an excuse.

Poor Thomas. He might have just been having a bad day. Yet this one situation has defined him throughout history as the great doubter, referred to as Doubting Thomas more often than as Saint Thomas. Do you know anything else about Thomas? Many people know only that Jesus appeared to the disciples when Thomas was out running errands and he didn't believe them.

Thomas is believed to have gone to India in 50 AD, where he reportedly converted dozens of Jews and more than three thousand Hindus by preaching the Gospel and performing miracles in the name of Jesus. He was known by many in that part of the world not as Doubting Thomas, but as the Good Thomas. It is believed that Thomas was murdered by Hindu priests in 72 AD. Some reports say it was because they were jealous that he had converted so many Hindus to Christianity, while others say he insulted their deity. Marco Polo was told in the thirteenth century that Thomas was accidentally shot by an archer who was hunting peacocks.

But the main lesson of Thomas' life was around faith and doubt. Men and women of every race and age have heard his story, but have we learned the many lessons this story reveals? Our doubts are ours for a reason: They have lessons to teach us.

Thomas was a skeptic who refused to believe unless he had direct personal experience. Until he could see and feel Jesus' wounds, he was not going to believe in the Resurrection. The kind of skepticism that demands the proof of experience leaves no room for faith. In matters of faith, certainty is a myth; one of the essential requirements of faith is the absence of certainty. If you can be certain, there is no need for faith. And yet the demand for proof and certainty has become one of the idols of our age, an idol that has separated millions from God.

Thomas, however, was open to the truth. Some people use their doubts to lead them to answers, but many more use their doubts as an excuse to opt out of humanity's epic search for truth. Blaise Pascal wrote, "In faith there is enough light for those who want to believe and enough shadows to blind those who don't."

It is natural to have doubts, but we have a responsibility to seek out the truth that will assuage our doubts. Raise your questions, but don't expect other people to serve you up answers on a silver platter. Doing the work to find answers to your questions is an important aspect of the spiritual life. Answers easily found are often easily discarded. Seeking answers to our personal questions and wrestling with our doubts helps us to build a more robust faith.

Doubts are flawed because they can never be fully satisfied. They demand proof, but they question any proof that is offered. There is no proof, evidence, or answer that will ever satisfy some doubts. Science cannot examine the supernatural.

Healthy faith asks questions. The important thing to keep in mind is motive. What motive is driving your question? Are you really looking for answers or are you looking for an excuse not to believe? The former will grow your faith; the latter will destroy it. Investigate your doubts by all means, but do it with a hunger for truth.

Perhaps one of the most important lessons that come from Thomas' story is a recurring theme throughout Jesus' teachings: Don't judge. Avoid the temptation to judge others, but also avoid the poison of judging yourself. Don't judge your doubts. Great faith and great doubt go hand in hand. Even the saints were plagued with doubts at times.

The stunning example in our own times is that of Mother Teresa. Declared by many a saint during her lifetime, and by the Church less than twenty years after her death, she was a light of faith and hope in the world. Yet after her death her private papers revealed that she had suffered from incredible doubt, and for long periods of her life she felt that God was absent. Using words like "darkness," "dryness" "torture," and "loneliness," she wrote about the spiritual agony she often experienced, comparing it to hell and revealing that at one time her doubts were so great that she even questioned the existence of God.

These were astounding and important revelations. Too often

we have left these types of things out when telling the stories of the saints, and that is a massive disservice to ordinary people like you and me, struggling to live our faith each day amid our doubts and limitations. Authentic faith is going to have to wrestle with doubt from time to time. It's important not to lose sight of the fact that this is natural, normal, and healthy.

The part of Thomas' story that is easily forgotten is what happens when Jesus returned eight days later. This is one of the great confessions of faith in the Bible. I can just imagine Thomas falling to his knees and saying with great sincerity and emotion, "My Lord and My God!" (John 20:28). These words have particular significance for me because they are inscribed beneath the tabernacle in the parish where I went to Mass every Sunday as a child.

Thomas' doubts led him to a conversation with Jesus and a deeper relationship with him. May all our doubts do the same.

· · · · · · · · · · · · · · · · · ·

JESUS,
I believe in you, I trust in you, and I place my hope in you. But at times I have doubts, I get anxious and worry, I think I have to take care of everything myself, and I can get discouraged and even depressed. Liberate me from my arrogance and fill me with humility, so I can live confidently in your love and your light.
Amen.

15. BERNARD:
In Search of Excellence

· · · · · · · · · · · · · · · · · · ·

Are you committed to the pursuit of excellence?

WE ALL NEED heroes; without them we wither and perish.

The older I get, the more my father becomes a hero. Born into poverty and prejudice, uneducated and unsupported, he lived an extraordinary life in the most ordinary ways. My father loved people and he loved life. He had an impeccable work ethic, was intolerant of ingratitude and laziness, and had a wonderful curiosity. People sought his advice, which was always simple, practical, and wise.

Even before I had children myself, I often wondered how he had managed to make his way through life. How did he escape poverty? How did he get up and go to work each day during the years he was underpaid and underappreciated? How did he pay all the bills? How did he so patiently chisel away at life to create the one he imagined long ago and far away, when he was cold and hungry as a child in London? All I know is that character had a lot to do with it.

There are two things about my dad that I think of time and again. He was always happy for people when good things happened for them. If someone got a new car—even though he never owned a new car in his whole lifetime—he was genuinely happy for them. If someone got a promotion or won the lottery, he was happy for them. He was happy for people who were successful.

Over the years, life has shown me how rare my father was in this regard. There is a lot of envy, self-centeredness, and jealousy in this world. Very few people are able to be truly happy for you when you succeed. I have learned this lesson painfully in my own life. It dawned on me a few years ago that most people are happy when you are successful, as long as you are not more successful than they are. But become more successful than they are and many people quickly become jealous and judgmental. I have lost more than a few friends this way.

My father was a fine man. I miss him.

The other quality he exemplified that touches my daily life is his love of excellence. He was constantly drawing my attention toward excellence. Whether it was in business or sports, the arts or politics, with a world-class garden or an incredible meal, my father was a lover of excellence in every arena of life. Terms such as *continuous learner* and *best practices* are commonplace today, but my father was a lifelong learner and an avid student of best practices and excellence long before they became catchphrases.

The saints are the kings and queens of best practices in the spiritual realm. If we study their lives and get beyond the plaster-cast statues and deep into their humanity, they will share with us the best practices they discovered and embraced.

Too often, we set the saints aside, saying, "I'm not like them." We put them on a pedestal and claim we are doing so out of respect. But are we? Is it possible that we elevate them on those pedestals so we can pretend that they are different, a special class of human beings, a super race, so that we don't have to strive to be saints ourselves? Our willingness to complacently settle for mediocrity is massive.

Saints are lovers of excellence. They are constantly learning more about God, humanity, the Church, Jesus' vision, and the spiritual practices that help them to become the-very-best-version-of-themselves.

My father's name was Bernard. His patron saint was Bernard of Clairvaux (1090–1153). Saint Bernard was driven and strong-willed, a charismatic leader who was supremely eloquent, and the most admired priest of his time.

Bernard was a French monk of the Cistercian order. The original emphasis of the Cistercian life was holiness through manual labor and self-sufficiency. The Cistercian order was begun by a group of monks who felt that the Benedictines had strayed too far from *The Rule of Saint Benedict* and who wanted to follow the rule more closely. Less than twenty years later the Cistercians were themselves in need of reform. This reform was led by Bernard.

Today anyone with a new idea is heralded as a reformer. Bernard was a reformer, but his reforms were based in deep study of history, the Scriptures, Christian tradition, and prayer. So reform is not simply trying out new ideas; it begins always with a search for wisdom.

The Cistercian order continued to go through a number of reforms, and in the seventeenth century a group of monks broke away to live a "simpler life." They would become the Trappists, and two hundred years later, a Trappist living in the United States would become the most famous in the world: Thomas Merton.

Everything and everyone needs reform from time to time. To reform something means to make changes to it in order to improve it. I need reforming; I know that. I need to be reformed again and again. We are told we are created in the image of God, but when I slow down to reflect I discover that I am constantly *de*forming myself into the image of something else. Over and over again, I find myself saying, doing, and thinking things that don't help me become the-best-version-of-myself.

Yes, we all need reform, or change for the better. Anyone can change stuff. But change for the sake of change is insanity, and not all change is progress. Change for the better is never easy, but it's always worth it.

Do you need reform? What part of your life most needs it? From time to time, everything and everyone needs a good reformation. How's your marriage? How are your personal finances? How is your physical fitness? How's your spiritual health? How is your work/career? Family life?

Sooner or later, under the weight of our collective complacency most things fall into mediocrity and become something very different than they were intended to be. The next question is, are you willing to make the sacrifices necessary to bring about reform? The thing about Saint Bernard is he was prepared to lay down his life for reform, to make something better.

Reform, renewal, transformation, and change—these are beautiful things when they lead to something that is renewed, refreshed, and improved. What needs to be renewed, refreshed, and improved in your life? Whatever you sense needs reforming in your life, God yearns to collaborate with you in that reformation. Do not be afraid. Be bold. Live boldly even if you are surrounded by cowards and critics.

· · · · · · · · · · · · · · · · · ·

FATHER OF ALL CREATION,
Fill me with a love of excellence, fill me with a hunger
for excellence, and make me excellent in all the ways
you envisioned while I was still in my mother's womb.
Amen.

16. THÉRÈSE OF LISIEUX:
It's the Little Things

. . . .

What list of attributes describes your best self?

THESE FEMALE Catholic saints never cease to amaze me. I have said it once, and I will say it again. Many of the most extraordinary women in history are Catholic saints. They were elegant and dignified, kind and courageous, confident and deliberate, humble and honest. They were strong-willed and at the same time had the beauty of self-control. They were incredible thinkers and prayerful giants. And their love knew no limits, as demonstrated by their empathy and compassion for others. Thérèse of Lisieux is just one example of many.

Saint Thérèse was dead by the age of twenty-four; she entered the cloistered life as a Carmelite nun at fifteen and died nine years later, yet few women have had more impact than the Little Flower, as she is affectionately known. She is the ultimate example of blooming where you are planted.

Toward the end of her life her superiors ordered her to write her story. Thérèse was reluctant; in fact, in the end her vow of obedience had to be invoked to get her to write. Those writings became the enduring classic *Story of a Soul*, in which she outlines what she calls "the little way." The essence of the little way is to do little things with great love. By pouring great love into the smallest act, Thérèse discovered great joy.

Mother Teresa introduced me to Thérèse of Lisieux. In the modern slums of Calcutta, Mother Teresa would demonstrate the power of the little way with the whole world watching. Both she and Thérèse of Lisieux felt called to love those who seemed least lovable. They searched for Jesus in the faces of people the world saw as unlovable.

Again, we are confronted not by complex philosophy or academic theology, but by the simple and consistent application of the Gospel. These amazing women took Jesus at his word when he told us that whatever we do for another person we do for him. When someone actually lives the Christian faith, it is practical, relevant, accessible, and hopeful.

Mother Teresa and Thérèse of Lisieux didn't waste their lives caught up in the self-importance of wondering what God's specific will was for them. They knew clearly what his universal will was for us all: to love others. By living what they knew to be the simple and universal will of God, they discovered his specific will for their days, weeks, months, and lives. Thérèse of Lisieux wrote, "Holiness consists simply in doing God's will, and being just what God wants us to be."

How would your life be different if you treated every person in your life as if he or she were Jesus? How would the world be different if we all treated each other this way?

The simplicity of the Gospel is powerful when it is actually lived. We have a tendency to complicate matters, usually in an unconscious attempt to avoid doing our clear and present duty as Christians. We tend to become paralyzed thinking about Christianity. Trapped by the inaction of theorizing, we neglect to live as the Gospel clearly calls us to live. The Gospel is an invitation to think differently about life, but more than that, it is an invitation to *live* life differently.

Thérèse of Lisieux lived an extraordinary life by doing little things with great love. From the cloister and the grave she has shared this simple message with millions of people. She is one more example of how God uses the most unlikely people to teach and lead his people. But how he chooses people for mission is no mystery: He chooses those who make themselves available to him—those who surrender.

Where do you think Thérèse learned such a beautiful, practical way to love? Where did she get her hunger to love God in an excellent way?

Born in France in 1873, Thérèse was the ninth child of Louis and Zelie Martin. Louis was a watchmaker and Zelie was a lace maker, and they both had successful businesses in their respective fields. It is interesting and no coincidence that both of these professions require extraordinary attention to detail and matching patience.

Louis and Zelie were parents to seven girls and two boys. Within three years, between 1867 and 1870, death seized a six-week-old girl, both their baby boys, and a five-year-old girl. Zelie described being left numb with sadness. But she got up each day, pressing on, pouring her love into her remaining children.

They say tragedy will either bring a couple together or tear them apart. These tragedies unified Louis and Zelie, intensifying their love for each other in a way that is nothing short of awe-inspiring. Louis and Zelie Martin were the first married couple to be officially named saints, and one hundred years later their baby girl would be known to the whole world as Saint Thérèse.

It is at home, wrapped in the tender care and affection of their mother and father, that children learn to love and be loved. This is where they learn that we are each made for mission and placed on this earth to make a difference in our own way. This is where they learn that God has amazing dreams for them.

The responsibility of parenting is enormous. It is often referred to as the hardest job in the world, and as such, it can be exhausting and overwhelming, and it requires tremendous intentionality. Parents often hope and pray that their children will grow up to be doctors or lawyers, or successful and happy, but I wonder, how many parents hope and pray that their children will grow up to become saints?

Louis and Zelie Martin, the parents of Saint Thérèse, raised a saint and became saints themselves.

. . . .

LOVING FATHER,
Teach us to do the little things of each day with great love by opening our hearts, minds, and souls to the reality that each moment is an opportunity to love.
Amen.

17. MAXIMILIAN KOLBE:
I Will Take Your Place

· · · · · · · · · · · · · · · · · ·

For whom are you willing to lay down your life?

IN A WORLD that can be cold, harsh, violent, and at times brutal, the saints prove that our humanity has a better side. Our better side is kind and caring, compassionate and gentle. The saints fostered this better side with daily acts of love and service, which prepared them for the moments of heroic selflessness that some of them were ultimately called to.

Maximilian Kolbe provided one of these moments—an epic moment of generosity—in the midst of the brutality of Nazi Germany, and he will be forever remembered for it. In the face of cold indifference, it was a moment of white-hot, glowing love. In the face of stunning brutality, it was a moment of gentle surrender.

Kolbe was a priest in Poland during World War II. After Germany invaded Poland he organized a temporary hospital in the monastery where he lived, with the help of a few brothers who remained. Between 1939 and 1941 they provided shelter and

care for thousands of refugees who were fleeing Nazi perse-
cution. This included hiding more than two thousand Jewish
men, women, and children from the Germans.

Eventually the monastery was shut down. Kolbe was then arrested by the Gestapo and sent to Auschwitz. In July 1941 a
man escaped from the camp. The deputy commander picked
ten men to be starved to death in an underground bunker to
discourage others from trying to escape. One of the men select-
ed cried out, "My wife! My children!" Kolbe volunteered to take
his place. After two weeks without food or water, Maximilian
Kolbe was the only one alive. On August 14, the guards killed
him via lethal injection so they could reuse the bunker.

The history of Christianity is paved with sacrifices large and
small that echo the love of Jesus' sacrifice on the cross in every
place and time. Self-denial and sacrificing for the sake of others
is another rich theme that runs through the lives of the saints.

In our modern times we seem addicted to comfort and aller-
gic to sacrifice. Both postures make the Christian life difficult
at the least and at most impossible. In order to love, and love
deeply, we have to be willing to give up some comfort and take
on some sacrifice.

Our willingness to make sacrifices for those we love is one of
the ways we give weight to the words "I love you." Consider the
question: *For whom are you willing to lay down your life?* Before I
had children, the question had a theoretical feel to it. As a parent, the question is anything but theoretical.

My sons Harry and Simon had surgery last month. It was a
simple and common procedure, but anytime general anesthesia
is involved with small children I get anxious. The heartbreaking part was spending time at the children's hospital. So many
of those children are never going home. They know it and their

parents know it, and it is utterly heartbreaking. You can see the look in the parents' eyes—bewilderment, exasperation, disillusionment, exhaustion, and other extreme human emotions. There isn't a single parent in that hospital who wouldn't lay down his or her life if it would save their child.

We hear the story of Maximilian Kolbe and it is awe-inspiring. Why are we so amazed? Is it because we couldn't imagine ourselves doing the same? And yet somehow we seem to forget that it is in no way original. Jesus taught Maximilian Kolbe how to take someone else's place, and he taught you and me when he took our place.

When my daughter was born I was beyond joyful; there were no words to describe my happiness. There is a special bond between father and son and there is a special bond between father and daughter, but they are different. I have tried many times to articulate it, but it remains beyond my grasp. As the fourth of eight sons, I had immense hope that one day I would have a daughter. We named her Isabel.

Saint Isabelle of France was the daughter of a king and the sister of another king. Although she was raised in the midst of privilege and power, she lived a very simple life dedicated to prayer and the poor. She had a deep love and compassion for the sick and the poor, and devoted herself to helping them.

Here we discover one of the fundamental truths about holiness and the saints: They are the most diverse group of people in history. Some were rich and some were poor; some were educated and others had no education at all; some had positions of power and authority and others did not; some were sick and some were healthy; some were young and some were old when they discovered that holiness is possible and dedicated themselves to it.

In this beautiful diversity we find a place for ourselves and no place for our excuses, so let us rededicate ourselves today to walking with God and collaborating with him to create as many holy moments as possible.

And if we are parents or one day hope to be, there is another question worth reflecting upon. Every parent has dreams for his or her children, but do we dream of them becoming saints?

We all parent toward a goal. Sometimes we are conscious and intentional about that goal and sometimes it is unconscious. Many parents focus on preparing their children for life in the real world, as it is often called. This usually means parenting toward a successful career and financial independence. Most parents will tell you that good values and healthy relationships are the things they most desire for their children, and yet these are often lost in the quest to help their children accomplish other things.

What are your dreams for your children? Are you intentionally parenting toward those dreams? Do you want your child to grow in virtue, become the-best-version-of-himself or herself, and live a holy life? Do you want your child to become a saint? Parents don't often think about their children living holy lives because it has been defined in such a narrow and restrictive way. It is often viewed as missing out on things, but nothing could be further from the truth. The saints experienced life to the fullest in a way that most of us cannot even begin to imagine.

Most parents are not called to lay down their lives for their children in one heroic act, but all parents are called to lay down their lives in a million small ways throughout their children's lives. My own parents modeled this for my brothers and me. My wife is heroically selfless in the way she ensures the consistency of our children's routines, the way she makes sure they have what they need, and the many ways she patiently helps them to grow and develop.

Everywhere you turn, people are making sacrifices so that others can live more abundantly—and we are each called to participate in that. We are each called to lay down our lives in small ways each day so that other people can be raised up in some way.

Maximilian Kolbe had laid down his life in small ways for other people thousands of times before that day in Auschwitz. You and I may never find ourselves in a situation like that, but each day is filled with opportunities to take someone else's place. Each time we do, that is a holy moment.

What small sacrifice are you willing to make today for somebody else?

. . . .

JESUS,
We all lay down our lives for something. Help me to lay down my life in a truly worthwhile way. So often I forget that you took my place and what that means. Help me to remember how much you love me, and fill me with that love so I can share it with as many people as possible in my one short life.
Amen.

18. MOTHER TERESA:
Truth, Beauty, and Goodness

. . . .

*How do you celebrate truth, beauty,
and goodness?*

WE STILL HAVE IT. This is ultimately what Mother Teresa's life announced to the world. Christians can still completely captivate the people of their time by embracing the profoundly simple teachings of Jesus in a practical way each day.

Just as the first Christians intrigued the people of their time, Mother Teresa intrigued the whole world in the last quarter of the twenty-first century. Her life announced to all men and women of goodwill that holiness is possible. Celebrated as a triumph of Catholicism by Catholics, but equally celebrated as a triumph of humanity by men and women of all faiths and those of no faith, Mother Teresa became a living, breathing, universal icon of holiness in an often cynical and self-centered world.

It has been said that people find their way to God via truth, beauty, and goodness. Why were people fascinated with Mother Teresa?

Truth. There was a foundational truth to her life that boldly reminded everyone that people were created to be loved, and that our love of others is not based on what they can do for us or what special talents they have. Rather, our love of others is based on the intrinsic value of each human being and springs from God alive within us.

Beauty. There was also a foundational beauty to her life, both explainable and inexplicable. The beauty of her smile in the midst of the world's worst poverty and her overflowing joy in the face of life's most desperate situations animated beauty in very real and tangible ways. This was especially apparent when placed side by side with the ugliness and cruelty we hear about every day in the world news.

Goodness. Her goodness became a worldwide symbol of selfless service in a culture obsessed with comfort and self-gratification.

So many people were drawn closer to God through Mother Teresa's truth, beauty, and goodness—and millions were drawn into a new relationship with humanity. She effortlessly highlighted how cruel and judgmental we can be to each other as human beings, but in a way that was not judgmental itself, in a way that inspired men, women, and children to love each other more deeply.

Through all this she accomplished something incredibly difficult: She reminded us of the truth, beauty, and goodness within ourselves. We may be uncomfortable admitting it. We may not know quite how to activate these things in our daily lives, but Mother Teresa and all the saints invite us to keep fumbling and stumbling around with the truth, beauty, and goodness God has placed within us. We may have neglected them and they may have been lying dormant within us for many years, but still they wait patiently for us to awaken them and put them to good use in our own place, in our own time, and in our own way.

The reason truth, beauty, and goodness are so central to our experience of God is because they are three things people never get bored with. We live in a time when people are gorging on entertainment of every type, and yet we live in an age of boredom. Hundreds of millions of people of all ages are bored. They may say they are bored at Mass, but the underlying reality is that many of them are bored with their own lives. A life that lacks truth, beauty, and goodness will ultimately become boring.

Truth engages the mind, beauty engages the heart and imagination, and goodness engages our very humanity and inspires us to love deeply. Truth, beauty, and goodness. Just four words, yet I cannot help but think they hold the antidote for our times.

An antidote is a medication taken to counteract a particular poison. What are the poisons of our age? Lies and confusion, greed and selfishness, violence and hopelessness, indifference and meaninglessness, relativism and godlessness, self-loathing and lovelessness—these are just some of the poisons that have infected our hearts, minds, souls, and society at this time. What are the poisons in your life?

Can truth, beauty, and goodness serve as the powerful antidote to these poisons? Yes. Absolutely. Without a doubt. How can I be so confident? Because what we are talking about here are not just qualities that human beings are capable of exploring and exhibiting; they are attributes of God. How often do you take time to recognize these things within you and around you?

Mother Teresa was a champion of truth, beauty, and goodness. She didn't have to wake up each day and remind herself to be so. She had a powerful set of routines and rituals that she practiced with unerring discipline. These daily routines and rituals were habits of the heart, mind, body, and soul, and they kept her grounded and focused. They reminded her of what mattered most and protected her from getting distracted, seduced, and mesmerized by shiny illusions.

What are the daily routines and rituals that keep you grounded and focused on what matters most each day? Do you notice the difference between the days when you are faithful to those habits and other days when you neglect them?

. . . .

JESUS,
You came into the world to remind us of truth, beauty, and goodness. Awaken us to the truth, beauty, and goodness that you have placed within us, so we can share them with the people we meet each day.
Amen.

19. MARY MACKILLOP:
Australia's First Saint

. . . .

How coachable are you?

IS IT POSSIBLE to be both faithful and critical? This is one of the enduring questions Christianity has grappled with from the beginning, though often unspoken. In a healthy community it is possible to be both faithful and critical. When a community or society is unhealthy and afraid, those who are critical tend to be accused of being unfaithful.

In Antioch Paul confronted Peter, criticizing and correcting him for not eating with the Gentiles. "When Peter came to Antioch, I opposed him to his face, because he was clearly in the wrong" (Galatians 2:11).

Paul saw plainly how Peter's behavior was negatively impacting the Christian community. He foresaw the repercussions of this around the world (and into the future) if such behavior was perpetuated and multiplied. Paul was a visionary in this situation.

Mother Mary MacKillop was Australia's first canonized saint, and when she was canonized the secular media focused almost entirely on one incident from her life. After MacKillop had founded her school and religious congregation, the community's constitution was approved by the local bishop. Several years later, the same bishop, under the influence of an overzealous vicar-general, sought to have the constitution changed. Mother MacKillop refused, pointing out that she and her sisters could be made homeless under the proposed changes. She was excommunicated for refusing, though an investigation later exonerated her. In the context of the times, as a woman in the late 1800s, standing up to the bishop and other church leaders as she did was a display of uncommon courage and boldness.

The saints weren't afraid to speak truth to power, and to speak it boldly. Too often they were punished for doing so and sometimes it cost them their lives. The great souls of every age have always encountered violent opposition from mediocre leaders hungry to grasp control and power. Beginning with Paul, the saints demonstrate that it is possible to be both critical of the Church and faithful to it and to God. Some people correct and criticize out of jealousy and hatred, but the saints did so out of a deep love for God, his Church, and his people.

When criticism is automatically considered to be infidelity, it is a dark, unthinking time. This theme leads most people to think about their rights and responsibilities when it comes to challenging people in authority, but it is equally important for us to consider how we respond when we are corrected. Do we respond humbly and accept correction as an opportunity to become a-better-version-of-ourselves? Or do we hang on pridefully to our old selves?

Champions love coaching. They love to be corrected, because they know it will make them better. This is true in sports, business, relationships, and spirituality. It is true in every area of life. Are you coachable? Some people refuse correction and instruction. This is a sign of massive arrogance and mediocrity. How coachable are you?

Mother Mary MacKillop had a great love for the poor and a strong conviction that all men and women deserve to be educated. The history books are filled with amazing women who loved deeply and served powerfully. I pray they can be a touchstone of inspiration for us all.

There is a natural pride we all carry surrounding good things that happen in the place we were born. That's why the Church has always been committed to celebrating holy men and women from every place and time. Your homeland, your city, and your parish need more holy men and women to celebrate. The people of your place and time need more holy moments to inspire them to discover their own capacity for goodness. Are you ready to collaborate with God in a new way and start creating more holy moments?

· · · · · · · · · · · · · · · · · ·

FATHER,
Your saints teach us how to live when life gets
difficult. They teach us how to endure all types of
hardships. We all have to grapple with troubled
times in our lives. During those moments of darkness
and difficulty, remind us to draw strength from the
examples of your saints.
Amen.

20. ANTHONY OF THE DESERT:
Be a Rebel

. . . .

Is the culture helping you or hurting you?

IT'S IMPORTANT to rebel against the right things, and Jesus taught us this with his words and actions.

Today's culture doesn't want you to become the-best-version-of-yourself. Today's culture doesn't want you to think too much about life. Today's culture doesn't want you to become hungry for the truth. Today's culture doesn't want you to develop your spiritual self. Today's culture doesn't want you to have a great relationship with God.

Modern culture just wants you to go along, be a good, obedient little consumer, and not ask too many questions about where the whole experiment is leading. I want to invite you to rebel against that. I want you to rebel against the modern culture.

Now, let's compare God's vision for you and your life with the modern culture's vision for you and your life. God loves you deeply and wants you to become the-best-version-of-yourself. The culture doesn't care about you and usually leads you toward a-second-rate-version-of-yourself. What drives God? Love. What's driving the culture? Consumption. Almost everything that happens in today's culture is aimed at getting you to buy something, or feel inadequate, or both.

Everything has a brand on it today. What did we first use brands on? That's right: cattle. What did we next use brands on? Correct again: slaves. Do we own the brands or do the brands own us? Are we still the consumers or are we being consumed? We need to start thinking at a deeper level. Are we cattle and slaves or free men and women? God sees us as his children. He created us free and wants to keep us free. The culture sees us as cattle and wants to turn us into slaves. Do you want to be a child of God or a slave to the culture?

The problem is most of us spend a lot more time listening to the culture than we do listening to God. *It's time to rebel*. Rebel against the things that seek to make you less than who you really are.

How are you being called to rebel against the culture?

Reject the world's vision for your life, because it leads to emptiness and misery, in this life and the next. *Embrace* and celebrate God's vision for your life, because it leads to joy and fullness, now and forever.

The history of our great faith is full of examples of men and women who rejected the culture's vision for their lives. Anthony of the Desert inherited an enormous fortune as a young man when his parents died. The vision the culture had for him was to live a life of privilege and luxury as a wealthy landowner. He rejected the culture's vision for his life when he heard the words of Jesus: "If you want to be perfect, go, sell what you possess and give to the poor, and you will have treasures in heaven; and come, and follow me" (Matthew 19:21). Anthony sold or gave away all his land and possessions, gave the money to care for the poor, and became a hermit. Over time he developed the monastic way of life, and he is now considered the father of all monks.

Now, this story may seem far from the world you live in. But reconsider it. Was Anthony's decision a difficult one? *Yes.* Was it a courageous decision? *Yes.* Did many of his friends think he was crazy? *Yes.* Did he have to overcome his own selfish desires? *Yes.*

Your world is not that different. When you decide to walk with God you will have to make tough choices, courageous decisions. Many of your friends will think you are crazy, and you too will need to overcome your selfish desires. You and Anthony are not that different.

Reject the modern culture and the world's empty vision for your life. Embrace God. You will be happier.

. . . .

LORD,
Help us to realize that the saints were ordinary
people who made themselves available to you.
Give us the courage to make ourselves completely
available to you, so that together we can collaborate
in whatever ways you envision.
Amen.

21. NICHOLAS:
Holding Christmas in Your Heart

. . . .

What can you learn from the real Santa?

AS CHRISTMAS approaches each year, something changes.

People become more cheerful and lighthearted, thoughtful and generous. In a word, as Christmas nears each year, people become more human. There is something about the spirit of Christmas that brings out the best in people.

Christmas today is a fascinating amalgamation of the birth of Jesus and the legend of a fourth-century bishop. There is something about Christmas that draws people, even non-Christians, to celebration.

Then of course there is Santa Claus and the question most parents dread: Is Santa real?

Saint Nicholas was an early Christian bishop of the ancient Greek city of Myra (modern-day Demre, Turkey). During his life he gained the reputation of uncommon concern for the needs of his people, and after his death he became renowned as a great miracle worker.

Nobody knows where the red suit and white beard came from, but Nicholas had a profound understanding of the method Jesus used throughout his ministry. When you read the four Gospels, you discover that Jesus almost never preached before he attended to some human need. He would heal someone—make the lame walk or the blind see. He would feed the hungry, often thousands of people at a time.

Jesus' concern for people's physical and material needs is one of the things that set him apart from the spiritual leaders of his time. He wasn't just interested in the spiritual well-being of people; he was interested in the whole person. Nicholas understood that. He understood that it is hard to listen to the Word of God if you are hungry and thirsty. He realized that it is even difficult to believe in God if your children are dying of hunger. Poverty has been an obstacle on the path to God for billions of people throughout history—and it is still an obstacle today. The saints realized that we each have the power to help some people overcome this obstacle.

The haunting truth comes by reflecting on two simple questions: (1) Is there really any good reason why a billion people alive today are starving to death? (2) How is it possible or acceptable that we allow one in five children in America to go to bed hungry each night? As Christians we are called to serve the hungry, the lonely, the poor, the uneducated. They are our brothers and sisters. They are Jesus in disguise; they are Jesus in our midst.

There are many stories about Saint Nicholas. They are stories of love and compassion. They are stories of self-sacrifice and great generosity. It's impossible to know if they are true, but if they are not, we should make them true with our own lives.

One of these stories tells about a widowed man with three daughters. He was old and poor. Having no money for dowries, upon his death, his daughters would most likely be sold into slavery or prostitution. One night while everybody was sleeping Nicholas rode past the family's home and flung a red velvet bag filled with gold coins in through the window of the old man's home. The father heard the noise and saw Nicholas riding off, and he spent the rest of his life praising God for sending Nicholas to them.

This is just one of many ways he generously interceded for his people, providing for their needs or giving special gifts on significant occasions in their lives. *Intercede* is a beautiful word. I love seeing someone intercede to solve a problem or improve a situation.

Religious leaders throughout history have a reputation for being disconnected from the daily realities of the people they claim to serve. This is why Jesus and the prophets were repulsed by so many so-called spiritual leaders. But Nicholas had the heart of a servant and was deeply in touch with the needs of his people. Out of this great generosity and thoughtfulness Santa Claus was born. Is Santa Claus real? Yes, and his real name is Saint Nicholas.

When I was a child, Christmas at the Kelly house on Beresford Road was always interesting. My seven brothers and I would sit at the top of the steps and elect someone to wake our dad. He usually sent us back to bed the first two or three times we woke him. Finally, Mum and Dad would get up and we would go downstairs and open gifts. It was complete mayhem, wrapping paper everywhere.

My father loved Christmas. He loved setting up the tree and putting up the decorations, midnight Mass, and Christmas dinner. He never got to celebrate Christmas as a boy; they were too poor. So he loved having his eight sons around the dinner table for Christmas. I can still see the way he glowed when we were all there, his joy was so great. He delighted in the presence of his boys.

It wasn't until after Dad died that I started to hear stories of the things he would do for the less fortunate. He knew what it was like to be poor and he never forgot.

Santa Claus comes once a year to our shopping centers; Saint Nicholas did something every day to demonstrate the generosity of God to the people of his time. Fifteen hundred years before Dickens wrote his play, Nicholas of Myra was already living out the central lesson of *A Christmas Carol*: to honor Christmas in your heart each and every day of the year.

· · · · · · · · · · · · · · · · · ·

FATHER,
Saint Nicholas brought the joy and generosity of Christmas to people all year round. Fill us also with the spirit of Christmas and inspire us to share that spirit with others every day of the year.
Amen.

22. MARY:
Beautiful Surrender

. . . .

What prevents you from surrendering
yourself completely to God?

THE SAINTS did things wholeheartedly. They focused their heart, their love, their attention. Too often we divide our hearts. That division diminishes us and the impact God wants to have through us.

Over the past couple of decades, I have spoken at many addiction recovery centers. Many of these places use *The Rhythm of Life* as part of their program, partly because I discuss in the book how we all struggle with addiction, but mostly because, of all my books, I think it is the best suited for anyone experiencing a transition.

Recently, I was speaking with my friend Tony, who has worked with addicts for more than forty years, and I asked him what the difference is between those who recover and those who don't. He sat there thinking for a few minutes, and then he answered:

"There are obviously many factors. The most common one you hear is that the person has to want to get better. But there is another characteristic that fascinates me and is very telling. Many of the people who come to an addiction recovery center are here because the court told them they have to, or their spouse said it was over if they didn't. Different people respond to this in different ways. Others are here because they say they want to face the problem, and sometimes that is true and sometimes it isn't. Our ability as human beings to deceive ourselves is tremendous.

"But the thing I watch for is this: Many people come and they will do everything you ask them to do for twenty-one days or however long they are here. I call this compliance. They comply but the main driver behind their compliance, their motive, is not recovery but escape. They just want to get out of here.

"The second type of response goes way beyond compliance to surrender. In my experience, unless someone is willing to surrender, recovery is unlikely."

It was a fascinating conversation. This paradigm applies in many settings, but especially to our practice of Christianity. There are millions of Christians who are reasonably compliant. They go to church on Sunday and participate in other Christian activities, but they never surrender to God.

Perhaps this is one of the defining differences between the saints and the rest of us: They go way beyond compliance and they surrender. They surrender themselves and their lives to God—and then amazing things begin to happen.

Mary is the perfect example of surrender. Her epic yes has echoed throughout history. Her yes was wholehearted. And the saints looked to her as a model of surrender.

I like to imagine Mary sitting with the first Christians. I am sure they brought questions and concerns, problems and difficulties to her, looking for advice and counsel. I wonder what she said to them. I wonder how she encouraged them.

Life is choices. We are constantly making decisions, and the decisions we make today determine who we become tomorrow. Are you a better decision maker today than you were a year ago? Making great decisions is at the center of the Christian life. God wants you to become a phenomenal decision maker. He wants to teach you when to say yes and when to say no. He wants your yes to be passionate and he wants your no to be firm. This is not only one of God's dreams for you, it is also the dream of every parent. Parents want their children to make great decisions. One of the reasons parents worry about their children is because they are concerned their children will make poor choices.

Mary and the saints teach us how to make good decisions. They counsel us to take the big decisions of our lives and sit with God and ask, "God, what do you think I should do?" They encourage us to pause during the day to consult God in the smaller decisions. With every passing year they aligned their decisions more and more with God's ways and will. But the biggest decision they ever made was to surrender themselves to God and his plans.

What prevents you from surrendering yourself completely to God?

. . . .

MARY, MOTHER OF GOD, QUEEN OF ANGELS,
Hold me in your arms and comfort me in
times of disappointment and disillusionment. Watch
over my children, hold them close to you, and protect
them from all harm. Share your wisdom with us as
you did with the early Church, so we can become
phenomenal decision makers.
Amen.

23. RALPH:
Love of Learning

. . . .

**What stimulates your curiosity and
desire to learn?**

IT IS IMPOSSIBLE to divide love; true love knows only how to multiply.

When my first child, Walter, was born I was filled with an immense love. I never knew I would love anyone that much. But then Isabel came along, and I was once again filled with that immense love. I instantly had as much love for her as I did for her older brother.

Having more children expands the love of a father and mother; it doesn't divide it. Where did all that extra love come from? In a way, with each child that God has blessed us with, the love in my heart has increased infinitely. It's hard to describe. You love them all differently, yet with the same intensity. And loving them all differently expands the way you love others. My eyes fill with tears just thinking and writing about it. I now know what it means to love so much it hurts.

My father used to tell my brothers and me that we were his treasure, but it wasn't until I had my own children that I really understood what he meant and how much he loved us.

Ralph Bernard is our fourth child and was named after my wife's maternal grandfather and my father. He shares his middle name not only with my father but also with my eldest brother, Mark, who was killed in a car accident ten years before Ralph was born. Ralph was born on Mark's birthday, a poignant reminder of the circle of life.

Saint Ralph was a Benedictine bishop in the ninth century known for his leadership and love of learning. Love of learning is one of the quintessential life skills. When we go for parent-teacher conferences there is one thing I always say to our children's teachers: "I don't care if my child is first in the class or last in the class. I am more interested in helping them to develop a love of learning. If they love learning, they will learn every day for the rest of their lives, and they will live rich and full lives."

At times it seems that modern education is a form of brutality. In Matthew's Gospel Jesus quotes Isaiah: "He will not break a bruised reed or quench a smoldering wick" (Matthew 12:20). To educate children requires strength, but it also requires gentleness. Their little souls need to be handled with care. We are all different and we all develop at different speeds. We all have different gifts, and when we try to force all children into the same mold it bruises their little spirits and often kills their love of learning.

My precious Ralph has a beautiful curiosity. As with his brothers and sister, it emerged quite naturally. Now the challenge we have as parents is to patiently nurture it.

Patience is one of the greatest lessons the saints teach us. They strove to be patient in all things, which reminds us that patience is one of the foundational virtues. How patient were you today? Of course, most of the saints didn't have toddlers to raise, and children have a unique ability to test the very extremes of our patience. We are called to be patient with others, as well as with ourselves. One of the areas we most need to be patient with ourselves is in regard to our spiritual development. It is so easy to become discouraged.

Continuous learning plays a very important role in reminding us to be patient with ourselves and helping us grow in new and exciting ways spiritually. The saints were continuously learning. They loved learning about God and the Scriptures, discovering the person he created them to be, and growing spiritually.

Do you know more about the faith than you did a year ago? How much have you learned about the spiritual life over the past twelve months? Most people are not called to a formal study of the faith, but we are all called to learn a little more each week, month, and year. For years I have been encouraging people to read five pages of a great spiritual book each day. It is amazing how much we learn and grow over the course of a year and astounding what we learn over a decade if we read just five pages a day.

It has never been more convenient to learn continually about the genius of our faith. Many of the saints never even held a book in their hands.

. . . .

FATHER,
Fill me with a love of learning. Make me hungry
to learn and grow in every aspect of life, especially
spiritually. Help me to keep in mind that when I am
growing spiritually, everyone in my life benefits from it.
Amen.

24. JAMES:
Do Not Be Afraid

. . . .

How often do you forget that we are just passing through this place?

LIFE IS A pilgrimage, but sometimes you need a pilgrimage to see your life for what it really is.

I have personally experienced the life-changing effects of pilgrimage, and I have seen this life-changing impact that a pilgrimage has on people of all ages. Each year Dynamic Catholic hosts pilgrimages to the Holy Land, to Fatima and Lourdes, to Rome and Assisi, and to Spain for the Camino experience. Men, women, and children of all ages join these groups. It is inspiring to see the way they bond together as a community of new friends, and it's amazing to see the way these trips transform people and their lives. I always know this is going to happen, yet it still amazes me. It is grace at work before my very eyes and it never gets old. Watching God at work never gets old.

There have also been a number of times when I needed to step back to gain perspective on what was happening in my own life and where God was calling me next. In *The Rhythm of Life* I spoke about the six months I spent in an old Austrian monastery just north of Vienna in my twenties. That was a very special experience for its spiritual impact, as well as for fulfilling my very human need for rejuvenation.

In my mid-thirties, I was in need of new perspectives again. This time I felt called to a very different experience. Many years earlier I had met a retired couple who had just returned from Spain, where they had walked the old road to Santiago, commonly referred to as the Camino. They told me about their adventure and I was immediately drawn to the idea of making this pilgrimage myself. It took me more than ten years to embark on the journey, but sometimes that is how God works. He sows an idea and it grows in our hearts and minds until we are ready.

The Camino is a five-hundred-mile walk that starts in the South of France, goes south across the Pyrenees, and then turns west across northern Spain to Santiago de Compostela, on the west coast of Spain. This is where Saint James, the disciple of Jesus, is buried.

Just before Jesus ascended into heaven, he instructed the disciples to go to the ends of the earth and preach the Good News of the Gospel to the people of every land. At that time this meant the west coast of Spain. The known world did not extend beyond there, and that is where it is believed that James went to spread the Gospel.

Since that time pilgrims have been making their way to Santiago, though the two most popular times in its history were the Middle Ages and the present day. In a culture drenched in hedonism and materialism, people are as hungry as ever for another path, a spiritual way.

We all need a pilgrimage—a journey undertaken for spiritual reasons—from time to time. It is good for the soul. Many pilgrims make a sacred journey to ask for God's favor in a particular situation, while others journey to a holy place to give thanks to God for some blessing in their lives.

Today I would like to encourage you to start planning two pilgrimages. First, I invite you to pray a little and dream a little. If you could go on a pilgrimage to anywhere in the world, where would you go? It may take you a few days to arrive at an answer, but once you do, start planning your pilgrimage. Even if you have to wait five or ten years for financial or other practical reasons, begin today.

The second pilgrimage I would like you to start planning today is of a local nature. In ancient times, people would make a pilgrimage to the nearest cathedral on a holy day. This may have required a journey of ten, twenty, fifty miles. With modern transportation, such a journey is easily accomplished. So, in the next thirty days, make a pilgrimage to a local church, chapel, shrine, or cathedral. Drive there, spend a little time in that holy place, and drive home.

As you make your way there talk to God—perhaps there is some special intention you want to bring to him. When you arrive, spend some time in prayer thanking him for all the blessings in your life. And on the way home, rejoice in the life you have been given—all the people, experiences, and opportunities.

There is something about travel that reminds us that we are just passing through this place we call earth. It is easy to forget this essential truth, and when we do, our values and lives become distorted. We are pilgrims on a journey. Life is a pilgrimage, but sometimes we need to journey to gain perspective, so we can live our one life to the fullest.

The saints made regular retreats and pilgrimages. These experiences tend to powerfully align us with God and give us the courage to press on. Otherwise it is so easy to become paralyzed by fear.

What are your fears? Why are we so afraid to love? Why are we so afraid to discover who we really are? Why are we so afraid to do what we love? What fear is holding you back the most at this time in your life?

Pilgrimages create a powerful connection between God and his people. They banish our fears and fill us with the courage we need to live the life we were born to live.

. . . .

FATHER,
Give me the heart of a pilgrim. Help me to be mindful of the fact that I am just passing through this place we call earth. And fill me with the courage to live the life you created me to live.
Amen.

25. ALL SAINTS:
Now Is Your Time

. . . .

How can you recapture the wonder of childhood?

THERE IS NOTHING quite like the beautiful, joyful, fun-filled love of a child.

My youngest, Simon, runs in and out of my office at home without a care in the world. After he has worn himself out running around, he crawls under my desk with a toy to play. Then when he needs a break, he will lie down, sometimes resting his head on the sheepskin slippers I always wear at home.

Sometimes I stop writing and just allow the feeling of his little head resting on my foot to consume me. I wonder how his life will unfold. I wonder what will bring him joy and what his passions will be. I wonder whom he will love and who will love him. And I whisper a prayer asking God to watch over him.

The name Simon has a rich and strong tradition. Saint Simon the apostle was one of the first followers of Jesus, and he dedicated his life to sharing the story of Jesus in Persia and Greece. Simon of Cyrene helped Jesus carry his cross. Simeon was the first to publicly acknowledge Jesus as the Messiah when he took him as a child in his arms at the temple.

Imagine these moments: Jesus inviting Simon to follow him. That was Simon's moment. Simon of Cyrene carrying the cross. That was his moment. Simeon holding the child Jesus. That was Simeon's moment.

Simon Francis was named after my second-eldest brother, Simon, and Francis of Assisi. I wonder what my baby Simon's moment will be.

The life of Jesus is filled with powerful moments, one after another, and it is easy for us to lose sight of just how powerful these moments were. And yet, each scene is an invitation to enter more deeply into the mystery of God and the mystery of self, the mystery of relationships and the mystery of life. But we capture the full experience of the Scriptures only by placing ourselves there in the scene we are reading. Only by imagining that we are there, in the situation, breathing the same air as Jesus, smelling the same air as the disciples, seeing the sights and hearing the sounds that were swirling around them, do we discover the breadth and depth of each passage.

Our own lives are also filled with powerful moments. Most of them come disguised in the ordinary events of life. Just as it is necessary to discipline ourselves in the habit of placing ourselves in each scene as we read the Scriptures, we also need to discipline ourselves to be present to the moments of our own lives.

It is so easy to sleepwalk through a day or even a week, then before too long we are wondering where months or years went. To be consciously present to each moment of our own lives is one of the most difficult quests.

What moments were you truly present for today? Which

people were you truly present to today? Or did your day get swallowed whole by a tidal wave of multitasking? In each moment, we are either present or absent. To do two things at once is to do neither. When we try to do two things at once we don't honor other people, we don't honor ourselves, and we don't honor whatever work or activity is before us.

On the first day of November each year we celebrate All Saints' day. This day is designed to remind us that most saints are not canonized; nobody will ever know they were saints. It is also designed to remind us that we are all called to be saints, in our own way, and in our own place and time. Finally, this is a day of inspiration.

People don't do anything until they are inspired, but once they are inspired there is almost nothing they can't do. Too often we forget this. We even belittle inspiration at times, as if it were less important than philosophy and theology. Pentecost puts a fairly large dent in that error.

Christianity is by its very nature hopeful and positive, and yet it's amazing how negative we can be as Christians at times.

The saints have been providing massive inspiration to people of all ages for two millennia. They were inspiring people; they lived inspiring lives. And their stories remain inspiring today. Perhaps it is because they demonstrate what is possible.

Somehow, they recaptured what it means to be a child and surrendered themselves to God, and amazing things began to happen.

Now it is your turn. Wherever you have been, whatever you have done, I firmly believe that God is inviting you right now to a very new and special period in your life. Will you open yourself up to it?

Set aside your pain and your shame, set aside any negative

feelings you have about yourself, set aside any self-limiting ideas that you or others have filled your mind with, and allow God to do what he does best: bring the best out of people.

Where do you start? With holy moments. Just start creating holy moments. One today. Two tomorrow. Six next Thursday. The world needs changing; everybody knows that. But we need to stop looking for worldly solutions to our spiritual problems. Holy moments are the answer.

What does the world need? What does our nation need? What does the Church need? What do your marriage and family need? What do your children need? What do your friends and colleagues at work need? Holy moments.

Holy moments are just what is needed. And if you and I don't create them now, then who and when? How much longer can we kick the spiritually rusted, morally bankrupt can down the road?

In every place and time God raises up people to create holy moments. In your place and time, God wants to raise you up. The question is, are you ready to collaborate with him, or are you comfortable letting life continue to pass you by?

. . . .

LORD,
Draw me nearer than ever before in my life, so that I can hear your voice and respond to your call.
Amen.

I hope you have enjoyed

It has been a great privilege to write for you.
May God bless you with a prayerful spirit
and a peaceful heart.

MATTHEW KELLY

Wherever you are in your journey,
you will feel like this book
was written *just for you* . . .

Are you ready to take your relationships to the *next level?*

Our God is a God of surprises and *new beginnings* . . . which do you need at this time in our life?

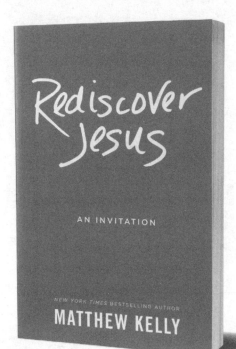

Have you fallen for *the lie?*

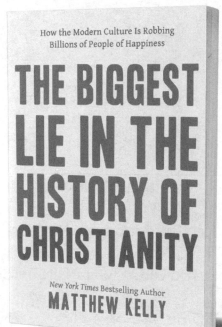

IN THIS BOOK MATTHEW KELLY
WILL TEACH YOU HOW TO **START CREATING**
HOLY MOMENTS IN YOUR LIFE!

• • • • • • • • • • • • • • • •

When you are done reading this book . . . pass it on!
That can be your first holy moment.

Let Us Feed You!

· · · · · · · · · · · · · · · · · · · ·

9 GREAT REASONS TO VISIT

DYNAMICCATHOLIC.COM

1. Free* Books and CDs

2. Amazing Events and Pilgrimages

3. BEST LENT EVER!

4. Join the Ambassador's Club

5. Check out the DECISION POINT video series

6. The BLESSED animation series for your children

7. Get Yourself a Mass Journal

8. Discover The Prayer Process

9. Take your relationship to the
next level with BETTER TOGETHER

 **Dynamic Catholic**